FOREVER MARKED:

A DERMATILLOMANIA DIARY

Cover Photography: Wayne Forrest
Formatting: Eva Smith
Revised edition, 2010. Printed by Lulu.com.
ISBN 978-0-557-18854-3

For all of the Dermatillomania sufferers out there who feel alone in their pursuit for answers and feel that they lack understanding from the world.

I have felt the same way, which is why this book is dedicated to my mother, father, and sister. Without you, I would not have been here to give my journal a proper ending.

Love: Angie

Contents

- PREFACE -

Originally I wrote this memoir for me, as a way to cope with the changes in my life and to inform myself about the confusing details of a disorder I have called Dermatillomania. The entries of this journal are day to day accounts of my experiences with this illness, from my struggles of trying to hide it from the public to the deep depression that accompanied my need to overcome this obstacle. I documented my journey in a blog that only I was able to read, but then I expanded it to a handful of strangers I met online who have similar struggles. Keeping this blog was my way of coping with life because I ignored my problems in the real world in order to survive.

If a person with this condition were to walk into a psychologist's office and get diagnosed, it would be with Trichotillomania. The definition of Trichotillomania is explained as the impulse to pull one's hair out; Dermatillomania is described as the urge to pick at one's skin. Both disorders are driven by the need to relieve anxiety through a compulsive act, but the current DSM only defines Trichotillomania as a mental health issue for reasons I haven't figured out. If I tell someone that I have Trichotillomania, immediately the person looks at my thick brown mane and sees that I have no hair loss; I also have all of my eyelashes and a full set of eyebrows. Imperfections of the skin are my

1

fixations but to relate my picking to the definition of Trichotillomania, I tweeze hairs out of my body that appear out of place to me.

Picking comes in many forms- some people find one spot on their skin that they focus their attention on. Me? I pick at the tiniest imperfections I find and do not give up until I "accomplish" my mission of relieving the anxiety of knowing something is on (or under) my skin that my mind's eye tells me shouldn't be there. For example, one of my routines involves perfecting my eyebrows. With scissors, tweezers, and a bulletin board pin, I will sit on my sink for hours trying to pull out a tiny black hair from beneath my skin. Once I feel the pull and see the encasing around the root of the hair, I feel a burst of adrenaline. For that moment, nothing else matters, but then I have to face the aftermath of bloodied skin and the scab that will form from removing the hair that is supposed to be there. As a rational person it's frustrating to try and make sense of this action because when it comes down to getting that rush, logic becomes secondary in my life.

A co-morbid disorder that some people with Dermatillomania have is Dermaphagia, which is the need to ingest the scabs that are picked off of their bodies. Some sufferers can also have a need to pick at a partner's skin. I am lucky to not have a familiarity with both urges despite researching them, so I am unable to go into detail about the drives or ticks behind both behaviors. Information I have found about these behaviors are only one-lined descriptions that leave me with more questions that answers. Is the need to pick at a partner's skin developed or already manifested through one's own skin picking disorder? What pushes a person to eat his or her own scabs- a compulsion or is it merely a routine (I am more inclined to believe it is a compulsion).

2

An ugly truth behind Dermatillomania is that its sufferers do not want to stop the skin picking behavior; this is one of the many shames that are hard to admit or accept because we wish that this impulsive act never became addictive in the first place. The desire must come from the cathartic feeling of purging the body of an unnatural entity. This disorder takes on many characteristics of other disorders: Bulimia because of the need to get rid of something seemingly toxic from the body, Body Dysmorphic Disorder because of the low self-esteem issues surrounding our scars, an Impulse Control Disorder since the need to act is overwhelming, and OCD because of its obsessive nature. It may be ignorance on my part but I wonder how closely linked Dermatillomania is with Tourette 's syndrome because of the need to act on an impulse; people with Tourette's are capable of holding back the urge but it becomes excruciatingly painful to do so. Not enough research has been done on this disorder to determine if, in some cases, someone's genetic makeup prevents her from ever being cured.

From speaking to people online with Dermatillomania, it's eerie how similar we are aside from the skin picking. I've noticed that we usually have traits of perfectionism, are introverted, have higher-than-the-norm intelligence, are extremely hard on ourselves with sometimes unreasonable expectations for ourselves and others, and live a generally conservative lifestyle despite being liberal and accepting of alternative lifestyles. Our awareness and high intuition helps us empathize with others, but our ultra- sensitive traits often hinder our abilities to accomplish what we want to.

On an average day, I will have accumulated about two hours worth of picking. Most of it is done in the washroom; I sit on the ledge of the sink and start on my legs, working my way up to my face. With every shower or bath I have, I am compelled to drive my nails into my skin to ensure the removal of dirt that a loofah or scrub brush would miss. When I'm not in the washroom, a lot of the picking occurs when I don't notice it. I will be watching television and tearing off scabs until someone in my family points it out to me that I'm doing it. Some mornings I wake up with blood on my pajamas or sheets because I will have scratched myself; the scary part about this is that my sub conscious desires have no boundaries because I have no control over these actions.

It's interesting to see how my writing has changed over the last few years. A simple statement such as, "It's very upsetting" has now changed to "I'm very upset". The subtle distinction between these statements is that the first one is emotionally detached while the second statement claims ownership of the feeling. That is one way I have grown since I started documenting this journey- I allow myself to be entitled to my feelings, even if they feel like they have no logic behind them. There are some grammatical fallacies that irked me to not fix, but I decided against it because I want this book to express more than information; I want my wording to be noted because it slowly changes as my thought process does.

So why edit raw facts and feelings while making this book? Some of the facts I documented were not about me and it is unfair to publish words that cannot be erased about someone who is important to me. I also gained information about Dermatillomania from trusted websites but without knowing how to cite sources properly, I did not want to get into any legal issues based on copyright. Most importantly, my thoughts were scattered! Although I attempted to make sense of them by writing

4

them out, sometimes they were expressed as incoherently through text as they were in my head. Instead of getting readers to decipher my cryptic language, I decided to refine my grammar to take the mystery out of my jargon.

Mental illnesses seem to lack hard scientific evidence behind the claims. They are diagnosed by observing behavior and psychologists listening to biased recants of memories and situations one was in; this is why there are too many skeptics in the public and unfortunately, in the health field in general. I won't make the common "Mental illness is like cancer or diabetes…" argument because it's not as straightforward to make the correlation between the illnesses. I would ask a non-believer to think of a time when he was overtired and tried to stay awake to get something finished. Would he be as efficient at completing it if he were wide awake? Is he able to stay focused on the task at hand? A common mind-altering substance is alcohol; it is known to make a sad person cry, a hostile person violent, and a happy person extremely confident or bubbly. While it is argued that deep down a person wants to express their feelings, alcohol lowers inhibitions and makes it difficult to keep a neutral composure. This is how simple it is to alter your mind, so how it that circumstances and triggers can't have a similar result without a substance inducing an altered state?

Many people wonder when it's necessary for them to seek professional help for mental illnesses because they don't know where to draw the fine line in what they can handle on their own. I know people who have issues with anxiety and depression but they are ok in handling those disadvantages in their daily lives. In my opinion, someone should seek help if a symptom is interfering with daily routines. Everyone goes through a rough patch here and there, but timing is also important to consider when deciding that it's time to get help in order to ensure that the problem isn't a passing one. With Dermatillomania, I am affected daily by not leaving my house when the aftermath is too visible to cover with makeup and when I turn down social events because of this insecurity. Another way I am affected is when I am late for school or work because I am too engaged with picking to notice the time, or when I don't get enough sleep because I spent the early morning hours picking.

My goal is to inform people about this disorder but more importantly, let closeted sufferers know that they are not alone. I went too long thinking that I was and it almost lead to my death. Life can be lived with this disorder- the challenges aren't too great to incorporate into a productive life, despite it feeling overwhelming at times. I don't feel weighed down by it anymore but it still bothers me that I don't have the courage to go swimming with the general public at a pool or wear shorts in the summer. Although this book is dedicated to informing people about what it's like to live with Dermatillomania, I need to advise that there are graphic images, explicit language, and potentially triggering content throughout this journal. In order to try to understand what brought me to the worst years of my life, it is crucial that you know where I come from. Maybe then health professionals will understand the severity of this disorder and learn how to effectively treat people like me.

- INTRODUCTION -

I grew up in Dartmouth, Nova Scotia, with my stay-at-home mother, working father, sister who is nearly three and a half years my senior, and a cute little Siamese cat. Growing up was a breeze for the most part: I would go to school, come home and play with my sister or father, play with my friends at the park, and spend time with the family. There were minor problems that I faced, but it was normal enough for a kid to go through in order to learn the tactful etiquette that socializing requires. I was an outcast who could never fit in with the popular girls because I had two contrasting identities: the tomboy, and the nerd. I would become extremely upset if I got anything less than the highest grade possible in any subject, even if it meant achieving a mark of 102% instead of 105%. I believe this mentality came from my need to prove myself more worthy than others because of my need to be special among family members.

The issue probably started out subtle but as the years went on, my need became stronger. I had always looked up to my big sis like most little sisters do, but I felt like I was always competing to be like her. There was no competition in my immediate family, but relatives were always comparing me to her. She was so delicate, almost to the point of fragility, had one of those perfect smiles you see on commercials, and knew how to naturally charm everyone with her big beautiful brown eyes. Her IQ had been tested at an early age, so it was confirmed that she could run academic circles around her peers. In comparison, I was... an awkward mess. My tomboy appearance included sweatpants, frizzy hair, a bit of chub in my belly, a pimply face, and long tee shirts. My demeanor matched my looks- I was loud, outspoken, silly, and couldn't sit still if my life depended on it! At school I was more proper and submissive to ridicule; being nearly a head taller than the next tallest girl in the class, combined with my "professionally unconfirmed" smarts, acne, and belly fat did not leave me under the radar from being teased by other kids. I was also unable to hide from the ridicule I faced from my relatives, especially from my mother's father.

I remember it made me feel so inadequate to be teased by my big and burly alcoholic grandfather. My grandmother died a month before I turned two, so my sister and I took on his new wife as a grandmother-figure. We never felt like she loved us- she was more of a friend who spoke of her blood grandchildren like a proud grandma would. She had been in my life since my earliest memories because my grandfather remarried rather quickly after my grandmother's death. My grandfather tried to show us love by giving us a dollar or two when we'd visit, but his behaviors didn't amount to a loving or gentle man. My mom believes that he was especially hard on me because he wanted me to be a lady instead of being... me. I can't pinpoint when the verbal abuse started, but it was a gradual process that became out of control when tragedy struck my family and we all fell to pieces.

Growing up, my father was the perfect dad. My sister was more of a "Mommy's Girl" while I was a "Daddy's Girl"- I was the boy my parents never had! He never tried to make me into a boy, but we had a lot of things in common with each other. Almost every day he'd come home from work and play badminton with me outside, or we'd play baseball with the neighborhood kids. We'd go bike riding, out for ice cream, and there were days he'd drag my sister and I outside to teach us how to change a flat tire if we ever got stranded in the middle of no where. At eight years old, driving was certainly not a priority in life but we faired the lectures on mechanics because it was time to spend with Daddy; I am now thankful for the lessons he gave us then because of how drastic our lives were about to change that would prevent him from teaching us in the future.

At ten years old, I still remember watching a music video at nine thirty am and getting a phone call from one of Dad's employees. I didn't bother to get the phone, but listened to the answering machine and heard the guy say that Dad had a seizure and was rushed to the hospital. I was so dumbfounded that all I could do was scream up and down the halls like a lunatic to wake everyone up. Once Mom got to the hospital, she learned that something more severe than a seizure happened to my father- he had a growing blood clot on his brain. That day marked the longest and most life-altering day of our lives.

After trying to drain the blood from the clot, doctors realized that the clot was growing faster than it was being drained. My mom was left with two choices: let him bleed to death or go into surgery to remove it and have him die on the operating table. She chose the latter because there was a chance of survival, but she was terrified that if he survived he would be in a vegetated state like his mother was after she had a stroke. Something that many people chastised my mom about was how she kept my sister and I completely informed about my father's condition, with no detail spared. In my opinion, that was the healthiest choice she could have made because it empowered my sister and I in a situation that no one had any control over. I am proud of my mom that she did not give into other people's recommendations that we should be kept in the dark until something happened.

Dad survived the surgery, but he was not 'out of the woods'. Every day, my sister and I would come home from school and go straight to the hospital to see him. I don't remember a lot about being in school during that time, but with having my father dying in the next city over while I solved repetitive multiplication questions I am assuming that I just wanted to get my ass out of there and be with him. My sis and I would bring a deck of cards and play on the hospital room floor. It was so cold and the room reeked of sterilization, but the most memorable part about the hospital was the sounds of the monitors. They would beep at a steady rate but we didn't know when the alarms on the machines would start beeping frantically and when we'd be pushed out of the room next. Is he dying? Is something else wrong? Why won't the damn nurses hurry up out of there and tell us what's going on?

Every day for weeks, we didn't know if we'd get a phone call from the hospital with irreversible news or if the last time we saw him would be our last. After about a month and a half of this hell, I remember being in the hospital room with Mom. It was no different than the other mind-numbing days but I looked at Dad and saw a mullet from when he was prepped for surgery, blood on his throat, a swollen and bruised face, with his legs being no bigger than sticks. I could hear the gurgling in his lungs that would be suctioned through his trach and it all must have become too much for me because I burst into tears. This man lying lifeless on the bed didn't have any resemblance to the father I had known my whole life, and that epiphany came to me when I looked at his now boney left hand and didn't see his wedding ring on. My mom was taken back by my outburst and all I could tell her was that he wasn't Daddy without his ring; she wasn't going to put it on until he got home from the hospital in case it got lost, but she was quick to put it on his hand to signify that he still existed in the unfamiliar body, somewhere.

After spending three months in a coma and three more months in rehab, he was able to come home. My mother and sister have faith that angels were watching over us when Dad survived, but I have always been more inclined to think that his nearly perfect health and large network of family helped him live through this ordeal. Any sign of improvement was nothing short of a miracle as he regained consciousness, learned how to walk using a leg brace, and learned how to talk again. For months we had been on edge with fears that he wouldn't wake up from his coma and if he did, we wondered if he would even know who we were. Due to the blood clot pressing against his left frontal lobe, he lost movement in his right arm, has limited movement in his right leg, suffers from short term memory loss, has no motivational skills, and has troubles with his speech. Personally, I would take him having this disability over the sentiment of visiting a gravestone.

Life changed drastically for the four of us and the roles of the family dynamic were reversed. My sister and I took on caregiver roles with Dad by helping him with his physiotherapy exercises and speech homework while a part of my mother had to learn how to raise a ten and fourteen year old alone. She always had a strong nurturing trait, which made her take on a caregiver role with my grandfather and the wife he was separated from, along with my father. When my sister and I had to learn how to grieve for a father who was still alive, we also had to learn how to live without our being our mother's top priorities.

Without stable adult roles in our lives, my sister and I were confused growing up. I will never blame my mother for not always being present because she did the absolute best job possible, given that there are no handbooks on how to bring up two pre-teens when your husband has an unexpected blood clot to the brain. We were immediately put into counseling to try to undo some damage and ensure that we would move past this unwarranted tragedy. I remember the first psychologist I had was worried about my anger and my "tough" attitude; he had told my mom that I was not dealing well with what had happened and that I should be on anti-depressants. At the time, my mother was uninformed about mental illness and the medications for it, so she refused to have me on an anti-depressant at such a young age.

My life was hell from the ages of ten to fourteen. In lieu of my parents' emotional absences, I was more subjected to my grandfather's ridicule. He lived in the same apartment complex that we do, which nearly made him a part of the immediate family. When we'd visit him upstairs, he would put out candy dishes or a bowl of chips and the minute I'd go for them he would rant about my weight and went as far as calling me "the human garb- orator". In time I was able to learn self-discipline when it came to food, with the inclusion of Thanksgiving and Christmas dinners, by seeing the twinkle of his eye while he waited for me to indulge.

On one of Granddad's last New Year's celebrations, he was drunk with his friend and decided to go off on me. I was wearing a dress that was starting to show some of my curves, and he proceeded to tell me that it didn't look good on me. I was still too chunky and he went into detail about how classy the dress was not. I was also wearing a fake tattoo on my arm, which he also ranted about, continuing to let me know that guys will only ever see me for one thing by making trashy choices with my appearance. He wouldn't drop the subject of me for a lot of the night, until I went back to my apartment alone to hear the clock strike midnight. His ranting was excessive- he was trying to mold me into a "seen-but-not-heard" lady and continued on his usual rant about how smart and pretty my sister was, and how I should be more like her. Even a decade after his death, my mother gets upset that I focus on the negatives of the relationship I had with her father; there may have been some nice moments, but it is easier to recall the eye of the hurricane instead of reminisce about the calm before the storm.

I had just turned fourteen when my grandfather died in front of my mother and me. His heart gave up after he had fallen in his washroom and we found out afterward that he already knew that he was dying. He had cirrhosis of the liver and did not take care of his diabetes; he had stopped drinking in the weeks leading up to his unexpected death and he was kinder than I could ever remember, which is what I want to believe was his true self beneath the alcohol. A couple of weeks later, I started to date a boy named Bobby who had a nine month crush on me and it ended up turning into a dynamic three year relationship. From that point on, my life was documented through recollections of teenage memories and current struggles. After being alive for nearly twenty years,

13

every wall I put up to protect myself crumbled at my feet and I was left to face with what my life had become- with who I had become.

- CHAPTER I: Explanation & Memories -

1 t's difficult to write about something that you have done for your whole life in some shape or form because there's too much to write about; so much of my life has been ruined. But is it that I have let this disorder ruin me and take over any possible happy aspect of my life or was I really just thrown into such harsh circumstances which (*for some reason*) led me to cope by self-destructing? Even if that sounds like an oxymoron, it makes sense because of the tension release that happens after I "do it" to myself. Many times, it feels like an accomplishment when I've dug into my skin so far, then pulled something out. Does it subliminally represent an accomplishment that I am not able to feel with other areas of my life? There are many reasons I've thought about why I do this, but it doesn't matter because whatever possibility I come up with does not account for the fact that **I. can't. stop. this. addiction.**

My most recent therapist, a registered nurse (since my social worker dumped me off), told me to just stop- that I'm capable of stopping whenever I want to. But that's like telling an alcoholic to "just put down the bottle". And not to sound like my illness is more serious than others, but as hard as it is for an alcoholic to lock herself in the closet and go through withdrawals from booze, what can I do? Wherever I go, I am with me and cannot run away from the culprit. Yesterday in the mail I received a pamphlet/ invitation from this registered nurse to attend a Self Harm Support Group meeting. It's a "peer led self help group for people 19+ who are struggling with their own self-harm". It's in the capital city of where I live, and the meetings are on every fourth Thursday of the month. The next one is May 25th... a day before my 20th birthday. I'll try to get that day off work for this meeting, but it'll look like an excuse to make sure I get a day off for partying, what most people would do to celebrate at my age.

Thepredicament I'm facing is that I fear I'll be further alienated from people who know about this illness. Maybe my opinion breeds ignorance, but slashing your wrists is not addictive; it's a stress reliever unlike the compulsive component of my problem. I have never had a problem with cutting, and I know that when people think of self harm, that and burning the skin are the only two ideas that come to mind. I'll still be the freak of the group for finding a creative measure of self mutilating. Instead of only trying to get help through online support groups about skin picking (*which I've been doing constantly*), I should try in person also. I'm just conflicted about whether or not to go...

Speaking of work, today the subject of shaving came up. The woman I worked with today wanted to see my unshaven legs, and I said no... for more than obvious reasons. While I was standing up and she was seated, she tried to lift my pant leg up. Such an innocent move on her part since no one would expect the sight underneath, but I jumped back so quickly that she didn't see. I've had to do this many times throughout these past seven years. I've been in several situations where people wanted to see my legs for whatever reason and I've had to make excuses or just tell people a bold-faced lie.

With the warmer weather approaching, I know it'll be hard to hear the questions about why I won't wear shorts and why I won't go to the beach, but I'll have to lie and say that I don't like to do either. Technically both lies have become true, but before when I just picked at myself as often as a "normal" person would, I loved swimming and wearing shorts. I still like swimming but don't get the opportunity to do it because every beach/ pool in my area is public. It's strange, but at the beginning of puberty my legs were the only part of my body I was happy with; everything else was so ugly, so why did I decide to lash out specifically on the only part of my body I was content with? Because of the social stigma behind destroying skin that isn't easily covered up, or because I want to look as ugly as I feel on the inside? I don't know... I don't know anything.

Remembering   *05-07-2006*

In my second semester of grade 12, it was thought that I had a skin condition called Lichen Simplex Chronicus. At first the dermatologist gave me a strong steroid cream that was to be used anywhere but my face because it is too intense and it would wear away at the skin. The cream didn't work on my legs and they ached so much

17

because it had to be put in the fridge, so it was like spreading a block of ice across my flesh and feeling the cold penetrate beneath my bones.

The alternative treatment was to go to an upright tanning bed-like contraption for a monitored amount of time. I had to go 3 times a week during school because it would interfere with work (*though I maintained a 90% average that semester*). The process was that I'd have to have a ten minute chemical bath and then go under the lights for a very short period of time. It was kind of cute how I was getting "medical treatments" and missing school for it, but coming back with a tan! The tans did reduce the scars, but of course the problem was only masked... and the scars remained from years of previous damaging/ mutilation.

I'm writing about this because today in my store, the manager of the tanning salon across the street came in to buy a pop and I talked to her about the deals she has this summer. I'll be buying a package because if I can tan away the damage I do quicker than I pick at my skin, then my self- esteem will raise slightly, which is what I did last summer. I know I'll never be able to wear shorts in public again and as much as I don't want to accept it, I have to. I just want to live to see the day where I can accept myself, forgive myself for causing my scars, and get my body to look human instead of a shapeless mold covered with tiny red disasters.

Tanning will not solve the problem, but while I wait to see the psychiatrist to get proper medication for my depression, I have to try to make life better. Although specialists tell me they don't know how to help me, I recognize that I'm addicted somehow behaviorally and I'm at the point where no pill will turn my life around. There has to be an underlying cause, something that's making me do this. Solve that problem then worry about actually stopping this, which will halt the damage done to my body and my self- image. There has to be a reason why, in grade 8, this got out of control.

Really, which will kill me first- skin cancer from all of the UV rays from tanning or the hate I have toward myself? I think I know the answer.

No Goals   *05-09-2006*

All I've ever wanted to be is a housewife. I was coerced and maybe even peer pressured into going to university in my Advanced English 12 class two years ago. The teacher made the class raise their hands if they were planning on going to university. I was the only person who didn't raise her hand and he proceeded to tell me (in front of everyone) how stupid of me it would be not to go. So I decided to go and take random courses of things I had interest in and hoped that I would find out along the way what I wanted to major in. And with what seemed to be a glimmer of hope, I discovered a love of mine. After taking Theatre 2000, a performance class in my first year of University, I made a goal to get into the university's Acting Program. Last year I knew I'd have a year and a half to prove myself, my dedication, talent, and abilities before auditioning.

I worked my ass off in that time frame. I took a dance class, contributed regularly in my academic classes, wore the proper attire, was in two school performances, made sure to go to every acting class, even if I was having horrible days regarding my depression or anxiety, and wrote in my daily class journal in massive amounts of detail. When it came time to audition, I fucking cracked by bawling my eyes out spontaneously when I forgot a line in my monologue. Then the panel let me audition again after explaining to them that I was under a lot of stress, but I knew deep down that I wrecked any chance of getting in.

Yesterday, a letter from the Theatre department was delivered to my mailbox. It was the rejection notice, the last nail being driven into the coffin. There is nothing else in this world I wanted more than to get in. Understandably they didn't accept an over-emotionally fucked- up twat over someone who doesn't crack under pressure. I'm not strong enough to endure any hardships. It feels like my fucked-up life is always teetering on the fine line of insanity, and that I was doomed from the start to fail at absolutely everything. I swear I tried my hardest to make a respectable life out of the shit pile I was given, but I still failed. Why even try to do anything anymore? I'm destined to be fucked over and even my hardest isn't good enough; it never was, and never will be. I don't want to give up but it feels like it's the safest thing to do. I've tried to think of accomplishments I've made in my 19 years of existence and haven't come up with a single success. I told myself that if I didn't get in after the 2nd audition, that I would be ok because the 2nd audition was the best I could do. The fact that I cried during the 1st audition and screwed up the only thing in my life going for me is what I'm beating myself up over. This is one of the consequences of life and looking at it from the panels' perspectives, it's safe to not have a destructive loser in the program.

Although having multiple mental illnesses has altered my life tremendously (well, not given me abilities needed to succeed) I now have to face the shame of telling all my theatre buddies who made it into the

20

program. The social aspect of the Theatre realm and acting was what I looked forward to. Now I have nothing because I was born to fuck up. I screwed my own chances over, but I didn't have a fighting chance to begin with. I finally found a niche, but it was never mine to fit into.

I'm so numb right now and I know the depression will set in once I hear "*I got in!!!!*" from everyone else. It kills to know I'm going into my third year while they are only going into their second year, but they have achieved their goal. They deserve it because of their talents, but I know that a few of the people accepted haven't done nearly as much in the theatre community, or class, that I have. I can say that with confidence but it doesn't matter because the fact remains that I failed. There's nothing left for me.

The Scars Always Remind Me   *05-10-2006*

While going through one of my many deep depressions, I decided to come out and tell my friends through an online journal what exactly was going on. It shocked many people who have known me for years, but I knew that the advice they gave wasn't relevant to me. Things like, "*You're pretty, what do you have to worry about*" and so forth. I know they don't understand, but it's the ones who try to understand and be there for me when I sink low who are worth confiding in. This was written before I received my rejection letter from the Acting Program:

March 5, 2006

"I never would have thought that I'd ever do this.

I have always gone as far as to tell myself that if the world found out, I'd kill myself, because I couldn't deal with the shame of being the only person who suffers from this.

But when you feel like your whole life has been hidden away, and you can't tell anyone why, you isolate yourself to the point where you think that nobody would understand if you told them anyway, so life is put to a halt. And when you finally feel like you have nothing to lose, when the quality of life has completely disappeared because of this one factor… you realize that you need to somehow set yourself free.

I'm finally ready to tell people the secret that consumes my life daily. Never did I believe or comprehend that something so menial could spin rapidly out of control and destroy my life. It hurts to think that it's been out of control since grade eight; that would make me 13 years old and I'm almost 20 now. No progress, just additional pain and self-abuse. This secret that has stopped me from living my life how I want to. I need to live again, learn how to, and know who my real friends are; to see who likes me for my personality, with all baggage included, or who only sees me as temporary company.

What is wrong is something I've done for as long as I can remember in some shape or form, as I imagine that most of you do yourself occasionally, but it got severely out of control in grade eight. I had just gotten into a relationship which lasted three years and my alcoholic grandfather had just passed away. I now find it impossible to be in an intimate relationship because who in his right mind could accept someone with such a horrific malfunction when he can find someone without a complex and destructive personality? Surely when people say "looks don't matter to me" while looking for a partner, you can get them to eventually admit that looks "sorta do

22

matter". For me, honestly, looks mean NOTHING; *how can I set a standard for someone else when I cannot even see myself as a person that doesn't amount to any standard?*

Because my problem is a newly founded disorder, it is still controversial amongst shrinks, which is why I was not treated for it when it first got out of control. No one knew HOW *to stop it, so they'd tell me this is just a phase and then talk to me about trivial matters like money and school. Still, no one in the area seems to know how to cure it but hopefully this summer when I go to into a 6 week day treatment program things will get relatively easier... even if the mutilation never stops. I have promised myself that I* WILL NOT *return to university until things are better in every aspect of my life because I'm tired of settling for less. I can't afford to go through another year battling this losing war with myself. Everything now is better than it has ever been in my life, but my real internal struggles aren't being dealt with, which makes it impossible for me to move forward.*

This disorder makes me lack a proper physical identity with myself, among other things. When I was a teen, it was thought of more as the normal self- esteem issues that all teenagers face. There are days where I still refuse to go to school because I feel too ugly and that no one can bear to look at me. I cannot chance getting a doctor's note for missing classes because the professors are all linked with each other and it will spoil any chance of getting into the Acting Program if I choose to go for it. But like all conditions, this has worsened and it seems nearly impossible to fix now since it has been out of control for so many years. I have tried everything I can think of to stop myself from further damaging my body, from slitting every fingertip of mine to attempting suicide (for other reasons as well, but this played a role). This is something I do to myself every day of my life. It's my worst habit because I do it for hours upon hours until my family physically has to stop me, after they realize I'm doing it... and it's how I cope with life.

It's called Psychogenic Excoriation. It has made me miss out on beach trips with friends, I've lost friends by having them tell people how much of a freak I am, and I've closed myself off from males (the dating perspective). I can't imagine a guy accepting the physical ailment to this OR the mental condition. Since I have to hide such a large percentage of myself from the world, I wonder if trying out for the Acting Program is even worth my time. It's been bad for the people who have found out about my condition accidentally by yanking up my pant leg, which I've freaked out many times before people saw the deformity... but there have been people including adults who have seen and looked at me in pure horror. A monster is what this illness makes me feel like.

I have had acne since grade three because I started puberty a bit early. That led me to being teased because no other child had my problem. By the age of ten I found out about the world of picking my zits, which I thought was normal; everyone pops a whitehead or two. It became a real obsession; I picked at any slight imperfection, a bump or scratch, and would make it bleed profusely. I know it sounds absurd, but I did it all over my body- my chest, upper arms, back, face (I dig pins into it to get the deep pus from growing zits), and legs. I also have a habit of scratching my scalp but I have only drawn blood a few times there. The rest of my body hasn't been spared of blood loss. My legs ended up being my primary target. This ended up destroying my skin and I ended up wearing pants everyday I went outside, despite the heat, and I had to make excuses for wearing pants all year round. I don't wear backless shirts either: the acne is gone but the scratching isn't.

By exposing myself, my innermost fault to the public's eye, maybe there are other people who can be saved before it becomes a problem. I know this answers many questions for people, like why I'm so unbelievably hard, critical, and unfair on myself. Even if it is impossible to get better, which it seems like right now, I want to raise awareness about this silent epidemic that has ruined much of me. While reading up on this disorder, I found out that apparently thousands of people suffer from it... but I've never met a single person who does. But how can I when we're all in hiding, ashamed of what we've become and how we don't have control over our impulsive actions? If you are my friend and are completely disgusted by me, then you weren't a true friend to begin with and maybe this will be what tells that tale and filters out what would be potentially harmful influences in my life later on. For those of you who went to high school and/or junior high with me, you never would have guessed since I kept this well hidden. No shorts or skirts in hot weather, though I have been questioned plenty of times. Even the university people reading this must be crapping themselves right now in shock.

Beauty really is skin deep and I'm just living in a cruel world, one that does not accept who I am and that is probably the most alienating part of this. Living life being your worst enemy is the most defiling thing possible because you can only rely on yourself to trust, so if you can't count on that one person... what do you have going for you and who can you trust?

So now you know how I'm ugly, and you have these answers. I was never lying, and now you can see that for yourself. Everything should make sense now. There is more to the story which I could write about, but I just needed to get this part out... finally."

Save You   **05-13-2006**

With thinking about Body Dysmorphic Disorder (BDD) and its connection with picking, I'm torn inside right now. It is thought that looking at a picture of yourself is healthier than looking at yourself in the mirror when you suffer this; the sufferer's eyes and perception through the mirror is distorted. But looking at pictures of myself, I still have the same negative views about my appearance.

The last few days have been hectic emotionally because I've had a really rough time with bad news, but amazing because I had a fun time last night at a concert of my favorite band. Sounds corny, but after a great talk I had to a friend as well, I now feel like I fucking cheated myself of a structured life. I'm left with this mess and I want to change it **all** around for myself. I can't reverse time, remove the damage already done. Instead I can try to make these rough days easier. But how?

For the last week or two I was close to giving up again. Nothing suicidal, but I've been so apathetic about everything that I was just going to let my pills run out and deal with the aftermath later. A few days ago I got my appointment with my new psychiatrist and hopefully he'll conjure up a cocktail not already tried and tested on me. I want one that'll help heal me, not make everything seem less important and/or relevant. I'm sick of feeling so numb, unable to feel pain because my world is in a fog.

I gained this newfound happiness by accepting some things in life. But I now fear that my will to stop picking will defeat me because for some reason right now I just cannot. It's as if I'm undeserving of any form of lasting happiness because of my diagnosed ailments. I want to resemble a decent human being, not even be pretty, but be just another "Plain Jane". When I look at that body in the mirror filled with pock marks, there is no way that it can be human or pure.

The pajamas I am wearing have blood spatters stained on them, both fresh ones and old ones that the washing machine couldn't get rid of. The bed I lay down in alone every night has clean sheets spotted sporadically with the depths of my self-hatred; it resembles a bloodbath more than a safe haven to turn to at night. And that's not pretty. I can't figure out if I ever had "normal" tendencies or if I've always been self-destructive since it's the only life I can remember. Has life twisted my train of thought into a dark hole or was I always doomed with falling into this sick abyss of emptiness?

I WANT TO CHANGE SO BADLY... but I do not know if I'm capable of it. I should be able to with willpower, which I have, so I don't know why I don't. Is it safe being destructive instead of being successful? It's cyclic- I want to change, but can't because I fear failing my own willpower. Being the person I've been for most of my life is exhausting, confusing, and depressing. Who wants to continue life "coping" so miserably in order to achieve a somewhat balanced and beautiful mind? Not me.

Hands in my Pocket   *05-15-2006*

Another work story...

I raised my arms to fix my ponytail. On a side note, a ponytail is the best hairstyle to have while suffering from this disorder because when my hair is let loose, I tend to scratch at my scalp, even in public, as a nervous habit. Anyway, the same co-worker who tried to raise my pant leg about a week ago noticed something- that I shaved my armpits.

Since it's not often I shave, it can get noticeable; but not so much to others because I wear dumpy t-shirts to hide the "spreading" scars on my shoulders and down my arms. So, the woman mentioned it then asked if I shaved my legs. I said yes in hopes that the subject would drop, but then she said, "Let me see". I refused again and she said she wouldn't believe me unless she saw it. I denied letting her see because I don't care what my co-workers believe, as long as it isn't the truth. My hostility appeared to throw her off but I don't need rumors floating around about me, true or not. She asked me why I wouldn't show her and I just told her I didn't want to.

My manager and I were working the other day when a worker from the mental hospital came in; she mentioned that she saw us smoking and gave us a number to call if we wanted to get in touch with someone for free patches and/ or free gum. I probed at the woman and asked her what other kinds of addiction programs were down there. She mentioned alcohol, gambling, various drug addictions, and the list went on. I whispered in her ear to ask about a self-mutilation one and she said there wasn't one but gave me a number to call. I think I'll wait until my psychiatrist appointment, which is June 12th. My boss was a little curious about what I whispered in the woman's ear but it isn't anyone's business what coping mechanisms I've wrongfully adapted, unless I choose to tell someone.

Then again there's the problem about what the self- mutilation "talk" is about-- just like I'm still contemplating going to the one on May 25th. Is it about people who cut or are there people like me who are actually addicted to other forms of self mutilation? Will there be people there serious about recovery? Since my job is relocating at the end of July, I'm going to quit and start some sort of recovery scheme for the month of August. I want to quit picking before I quit smoking because that's a harder task and, contrary to scientific evidence, it is more life threatening to me.

Will We Ever Get Out of Here?   05-15-2006

For the past few years, the summer has been depressing because of how jealous I am of everyone. As naive as that may sound since I do not know what other people are struggling with, I am superficially jealous of what I see because I know what they aren't struggling with. Today got hot around 4pm and I looked around at the customers in my store... ...they were wearing tank tops, shorts, or skirts. When I look down at myself, I'm wearing the same outfit that I do in the winter- baggy blue jeans and my faded yellow cartoon tee shirt. It will become noticeable, for yet another summer, that I'm wearing clothes inappropriate to what the weather is calling for. I'm jealous of the teenagers who come in because they have no clue how lucky they are for only having normal self esteem issues, not issues of being self- conscious about scars that they made themselves.

While working, I just happened to glance over at one of my co-workers when she was doing the end-of-the-night paperwork. It's creepy, but whenever I can slip a look at a person's wrists, I'll do it. I want to see that I'm not the only self- destructive person out there, even if I don't slash my wrists. She had about six whitened, slightly protruding, straight lines parallel to each other on her left wrist. I didn't mention that I noticed it, but it explains why she wears sweaters all the time. She has a similar mask on her that I do; this is the woman who has asked me about my legs a few times. If I mentioned to her how I noticed her wrists, it may reveal plenty about myself- my past and present. Work isn't the place for that sort of intimate socializing. I'm there to be a peacekeeper and get

29

things done- not to publicly alienate myself, which would add to the isolation I face daily from myself.

Made to Heal   05-16-2006

If you knew you were going to die tomorrow, would you feel like you have lived to your fullest potential? Would you have any regrets- not say anything that you wanted to out of mediocre fears of continued pain or rejections? Would you feel content in knowing that you have accomplished something of relevance, whatever "relevance" means to you? Or would you feel incomplete because you haven't left any sort of mark in this world except for the polluted air that you contribute to daily by smoking? Could you leave this world knowing that every day of your life has been lived to its very best, making people around you happy and bringing out the best in them?

It's impossible to realize how decrepit your mind and thoughts are until something inside your brain clicks and changes your outlook on many situations. This epiphany would scare anyone, but it is terrifying to me because I see how I've let things deteriorate in my life; my friends, family, health, and the overall satisfaction that is needed to be motivated to live. I forget what it's like to just let loose and be myself completely, to embrace the positives in this world instead of always dwelling on the negatives.

So what if I didn't get into the Acting Program? Deep down if I want to be a stage performer, I'll find other ways to achieve that goal. Not getting accepted gives me the freedom to choose if I want to further my education at university or take time off to get my life on track. Hell, if I finish a bachelor's degree with a major in Theatre Studies, it might inch my way back into performing. I'll need to figure out how seriously I want it, or see if I really want it at all; maybe I only wanted it because it was the first opportunity I could leech on to. Or maybe, because of the scars I have, I know deep down that this wasn't ever a goal I could attain.

After hours of research, I've concluded that my province does not have resources I need no matter how hard I try to get better. I don't want to keep trying and continue this cycle of failure just because there is no hope here; that will lead to continuous bouts of frustration and self-blame. Change has been needed for so long now because if I were to summarize the last 7 years, it would be far from fluff. I take ownership in much of it because I could have made different choices but instead of dwelling on what I should have done, I now have the responsibility to do what I know is right. I'm still driven, even if my past has bitten me in the ass and prevented me from experiencing success. But again it is my fault since I repeatedly neglected responsibilities that turned into extra baggage later on. I needed the excitement I got at the concert to remind myself of what I take for granted, how selfish it is to fret about the negative, that it's still possible to have **fun**, and to focus on making everyone around me see the best. I don't know what my next step is, but it's relieving to recognize that there are other options in life other than doing what is expected of you based on your age and intelligence (meaning, university). What the *hell* am I doing with my life?

Academics have never been my priority. I have only ever strived for happiness and I hoped to find it in a particular academic goal, but I didn't. That doesn't mean that happiness doesn't exist or that it doesn't arrive unexpectedly and/or in strange forms. All I've wanted for my friends, my family, and myself is to have the most complete and fulfilled life possible; to be satisfied, to overcome obstacles and inner demons, and to be at peace. Thinking about how I've been living almost half of my life is nauseating, but I refuse to accept that it's too late. I've learned this year that communication is crucial to human interaction- one must toss away insinuations, grow closer to amazing people, and find common ground with another.

I can turn this all around. Instead of driving down this dark tunnel, it's possible to reverse the direction or at least park myself to avoid any incoming traffic. The damage that has been done can never be reversed but I'd accept that in time if change starts now. I want to help others, listen to people, give advice, and share my own trials / tribulations / thoughts. We are all inspirational in our own ways, even if we don't realize it. For whatever reason, we've all been placed on this earth and we all have unique destinies- no one has a fate that is fabricated based on what society wants us to be.

As easy as it is to stay angry at things that have happened, they must be let go. What's done is done and cannot be changed. If you don't let it go, you can become a bitter old shrew, untrusting of people, untrusting of everyone's motives. Forgive but never forget because forgetting would mean to omit any lessons you have learned. Your quality of life isn't worth sacrificing due to your insecurities, even if they are justified. Forgive people for their ignorance, for their lack of judgment because you can't change others... you can only change yourself.

It doesn't matter how low you may feel in one moment because there's always hope. You can go searching feverishly for it or let it slap you in the face but always remember that whatever it is you suffer, you never have to suffer it alone. It's the lack of communication in this world that makes people feel so dismal, insecure, and alone. We all have lost ourselves at one point and to what extent I don't know, but I do know that there is always a light at the end of the tunnel... even if there are potholes along the way.

Baby Skin Tattoo   05-17-2006

I've always wanted a tattoo because I have a fascination with body modification. I've never found anything of significance until a few months ago and I never wanted to place something permanently on my body unless I was certain it held long-lasting significance for me. I'm intent on eventually getting twin tattoos of wings on my upper back; something simplistic, white, maybe with flames on it.

I won't get them until I have stopped picking my skin. First of all, I want to be able to show off my tattoo with pride, without having to worry about fresh war wounds. I can already see that near my shoulder blades there is a patch of untouched skin, which is where I hope to get them. I haven't found a sketch of the image I have in my head and I can't draw, but I won't worry about this until I actually conquer- and deserve- to pamper myself. It's a gift I need to earn or else I won't be able to appreciate the meaning behind it and it wouldn't represent a battle won.

It's also one of my motivations to stop picking; a smaller drive, of course, but a drive nonetheless.

Wings represent that I have flown out of my hell, overcome my biggest personal obstacle. Coincidentally, I am double-jointed in the shoulder blades so the wings would signify the wings I have when I pop my shoulder blades out of place. I'm thinking of having flames on the tips of the wings because I have always had a fascination with flames and this would signify that I have a fire that will never burn out.

With such motivation and finally something to be proud of on my body, I think my self-esteem would lift... or actually become present. But in order for me to stop this self-mutilation I think I'd have to tackle my psychological symptoms first, which could potentially put me in a more mentally mature frame of mind.

Last "Sexual" Experience   05-19-2006

February of 2005 was the worst month of my life. Bad choices were made, and consequences were dealt out accordingly.

I was at a friend's house one night during Spring Break and she invited a boy over who she really liked, and who liked her back. I had only met him a few times before then when he had dated someone I knew in high school. I don't want relive the details of this, but at night my friend crawled into her bed with her other female friend while he climbed into her parent's bed where I was staying. Nothing happened until 9am the next morning. Writing this out is painful... but I think I need to make sense of how I handle situations.

He showed no interest in me the night before, and the feeling was mutual for me... I hardly knew him, for beginners. When he was on top of me and tried to pull down my pants, the only thing swirling in my mind was to get out. I was petrified of how he would be able to see my legs, my scars, instead of being scared that he'd steal my virginity.

Since I have never been in that type of sexual domineering situation before, it made me freeze and I tried to talk my way out of everything that was happening. Still, I feel disgusted for not acting until I did, how I to tried and be nice about my rejection toward his forceful advances. It's so damn twisted that while this went on, my priorities weren't straight. My main worry was that I would be figured out for a freak. Initially, I didn't understand why he wanted to try to sleep with me since I wasn't wearing makeup, though it doesn't exactly make me "pretty" anyway.

Now I know why. I was just the person he could try to get with the easiest. I was trapped on that bed, under his arms and boozed breath, while his lips traveled up and down parts of me that I have not let anyone touch since. He didn't think I was pretty, though it really doesn't matter to me if he did. I made myself a target that night and I own that fact more than a year later. I should not have smoked pot, which altered my reaction time, and shouldn't have slept over the night without knowing the male in the house.

I thought this story held relevance in telling because my thoughts were fixated on what *could* happen if he saw the scars, instead of the fact that it was a traumatic experience. He would've jumped off of me, which is what I wanted, but it's sick that it would be under those circumstances. I beat myself up over what happened, how I tried to rationalize with him at first to stop, and how long it took me to get out of that situation. Things happened that morning that I have yet to tell anyone in my life and probably never will.

Time- Log   05-20-2006

With today's post, I was going to keep therapeutically trying to talk about my past and why it could have possibly led me to this point of addiction. Instead, there are a few events I want to talk about that occurred today during my 9am- 6pm shift at work.

1.   While working with the woman who has cuts on her left wrist, she started talking to me about how someone had come in a few days ago and asked her if she had tried to kill herself by slashing her wrists. She told me that she was offended by the question because she would never be "daft" enough to do something like that. She explained to me that she received those scars when she went through a screen window. I admitted to her that I noticed the scars on her before but never gossiped to our other co-worker or thought about bringing up such a subject. She told me she was shocked about how I could think that she would do something like that, but said it in a way like she looked down on self-injurers. I can tell she has an awful and most likely ignorant view on mental illness and is caught up with the social stigma about it. She said she'd be straight-up honest with me if she had purposely cut herself, but I don't believe her. I told her that even if she did and didn't want to tell me that I wouldn't look down on her for it, but she jumped much too quickly to her own defense for her story to ring any truth.

I didn't tell her I didn't believe her because it's not my business to know. Also, we are only co-workers, even if we do get along. It's obvious that I have some demons in my closet that I need to keep hidden from the public, so I assume from fragments of stories I hear from both co-workers that they certainly haven't had it easy and may have stories of their own up their sleeves- no pun intended. I wouldn't dare tell either of them about my picking. From seeing my employee's whitened scars, I know they are from slashing because of how articulate, calculated, and deep they are.

2.   I decided that I needed to act on trying anything to get better, even if it is a temporary fix. During my 15 minute break I went over to the tanning salon and bought a package. I'm actually excited because if I go tanning before noon I get charged for only half of the minutes I'm in there for; I bought a package of 100 minutes for $30 so in theory if I used up my 100 minutes I'd still have an extra 100 minutes to use. I feel conceded since I'm looking forward to this short-term way of minimizing my scars and close opened wounds. Tomorrow is my first day and I'm going right before my shift, but I'll settle for a temporary fix instead of the hopelessness I feel everyday looking the way I do.

3.   During my day I'm serving customers, like usual. This overly cheery woman came into the store and was being friendly with my co-worker and me while I served her. This lady scares the three of us workers every time she comes in with her chipper ness and we don't know if it's because we're bitter or because she's on drugs… or needs to be on drugs! While I was bagging her purchase, she looked at me and said: "*I don't want to offend anyone here, but (*she looks at me*) when I was your age sweetie, I had the same problem as you on your face. Do you wash your face with*

soap? (I nod because I'm too thrown off and embarrassed*) You shouldn't because it ruins your skin* (then she rambles on a bit more and I'm in a daze, just dumbfounded*). It's too bad since you would have such a pretty face"*.

Ouch. And ouch. My co-worker was sympathetic about it and actually said today my face looked better than other days. During the spout with the customer, I blurted out that I don't have acne- but I have a condition called Lichen Simplex Chronicus... which was the condition I was originally diagnosed with. It was an automatic response to defend myself from being accused of having acne, which I did have from grade three to high school. I can't believe I offered personal information to stand up for myself. I explained a bit more in detail about the condition to my co-worker when the customer left, but left out key details. I said that I'm always in a bit of pain, but didn't explain that the pain was emotional but led my co worker to believe it was my actual skin. I told her about the tanning and why it's important to me- because it reduces the pain and minimizes the scars, which is true, but misleading. Then I told her how this came back to our original conversation about how it's rude and intrusive to ask others about their scars, which is why I had never asked her about hers. Though I'm open-minded, open about talking about things in public when approached, I have my limits and respect that everyone has such diverse backgrounds. No one should dare barge in on it when they are not truly interested in your well- being.

It was quite an emotionally exhausting day that tied up some loose ends. Right after that incident I had to go outside and have a smoke before I got increasingly angry at the woman and about the situation. How **DARE** someone treat me as if I am ignorant about my own well- being? She doesn't know the years I've went through with dermatology treatments, nor does she know the plain truth that I don't even suffer from acne.

After working a nine hour shift and having to continue to hide my dirty laundry, I was glad when the clock struck 6pm. To get away from the rough circumstances from this cruel and taunting public is what I look forward to, but today was worse than usual.

Methods of Madness   *05-22-2006*

The tan today felt liberating. Even if I did have to go to work afterward, it's such a confidence booster to know that I'm actively trying to get my skin clearer. Temporary fix, yes, but it's better than nothing. And perhaps this summer I'll also get some sort of therapy down here (*though I'm highly doubtful since the mental health district has pushed me away many times*) to make it easier to stop picking.

I have attempted to stop picking in these past few years, but nothing has ever worked. Here's a list of what I've tried and why it hasn't worked.

What I've Done:

1.   <u>Cut my nails</u>- but then they became too sharp when I picked, so I filed them down and they went back to normal.

2.   <u>Grown my nails</u>- to make it difficult to pick, but my nails always break off.

3.   Fake nails- leave large imprints on the area I pick, which causes larger spots.

4.   Cream- a refrigerated dermatological cream that's supposed to speed up the healing process of sores. Doesn't work fast enough to keep up with the amount I pick at my skin.

5.   Tanning- with hospital treatments when I had my false diagnosis, last summer in a salon, and now in a salon. It's only a temporary fix to the problem.

6.   Cutting- I got the "genius" idea of slicing every fingertip of mine so that a surge of pain would go up my fingers every time I picked, resulting in me not wanting to pick. Also I fought the pain of my fingertips in order to pick; though it was working for a few days, it didn't last.

7.   Antibiotics- Pill form for over a year which did nothing, it was supposed to prevent infections from forming under and on my skin.

8.   The Sign- My sister and I made a sign from magazine clippings to be inspirational. Since we aren't able to remove the bathroom mirror, we placed this homemade sign over it so I can't see my reflection to pick at my face and arms. It's useless because I go into my parent's bathroom when I am overwhelmed with anxiety and pick there.

9.   Willpower- When the sign was up, I would consciously look up at the ceiling to not look at my legs while on the toilet so that I couldn't see anything to pick at. That wore me out emotionally.

10.   Anti-depressants- For skin- picking and depression/ anxiety, I've been on seven SSRI's. Only one has ever balanced my depression during my senior year in high school; because I never stopped picking while on it, the medication was ignorantly changed to try and "cure" my picking. I

have a new psychiatrist appointment on June 12th and with my new diagnosis of Borderline Personality Disorder, I may be thrown on an anti- psychotic.

11.   Therapy- As a teen the psychologists just passed this off as a phase. I found out recently that through all of my teen years, this problem was NEVER recorded in my psychiatrist's or psychologists' records. Ouch.

12.   Smoking- It sounds so skewed, but I tried to transfer this addiction to smoking. Both are self-destructive, and now I'm stuck with them.

13.   Shaving- I let my leg hair grow long so that there are less ingrown hairs to try and pull out of my skin.

14.   Hygiene- keeping it up to par. Exfoliating and cleansing the skin; I used to put rubbing alcohol on wounds to disinfect them.

15.   Support Groups- Online ones to find common ground with people, to know I'm not alone. I'm going to my first self injury meeting May 25th, which I'm nervous about because I've never opened up to the public about this shameful addiction.

16.   Suicide- For other reasons too, but a lot of stress, anxiety, depression, and shame come from this disorder; how alienating it is and how it prevents me from being who I want to be.

What I Haven't:

1.   Hypnosis- Way too expensive and not guaranteed.

2.   AA 12 step program- A recommendation I found online to deal with addictions but I highly doubt that a sponsor would recognize this as

an illness, so I'll save the embarrassment.

3.   Geography- I haven't looked outside of my province or Canada for help, but I'm working on it.

4.   Music- it was suggested that I put on music while picking and have bad songs play every 2nd song so that I'll have to get up as a distraction to change the song. The problem is about 85% of my picking takes place in the bathroom where there are no electrical outlets.

I probably sound like a typical low self-esteemed kid by saying this, but I've always told myself that if I overcome this disorder I'll get laser surgery to minimize the scars. What's awful is that with any disorder or addiction, there can be relapses. I never realized how hard I've tried to stop until I look at my "what I've tried" list, so it's a bit upsetting. Even with these gimmicks tried and tested, I am still in the same place as before, if not worse physically. Emotionally, I am still driven.

Those Were Not the Days   05-23-2006

While I'm in a depressed mood right now, I decided that it'll be the best time to write about what I'll call "*boy situations*" and how this disorder has affected me relationship- wise and interpersonally.

When the picking got out of control, it was during the summer of grade eight, which would have made me freshly fourteen. Surprisingly it got out of control around the time I started dating this guy named Bobby. We had started going out only a few weeks after my alcoholic grandfather died suddenly, so I'm still trying to figure out what factor was the main trigger to actually turn regular picking into a disorder.

Bobby was a loner and older than everyone in our class. He was always made fun of, had no friends, drove thumbtacks into his body, smashed his head on lockers, and burned himself. He liked me and pursued me for nine months until I gave in because I found common ground with him. He used to hang out in my neighborhood, which irked me when I didn't like him, but I eventually felt a connection between us.

It was a first relationship for both of us. He treated me like a queen by buying me things and showering me with hugs and kisses, but slowly I noticed I was losing my friends because they didn't like him. That summer I remember there were a few days I could wear shorts but it depended on how bad the scars were. By the time I entered grade nine, the Dermatillomania was full-blown and I depended on him for comfort. There would be days we'd be lying on my bed and I'd cry about the scars all over my body but he told me it didn't matter because I was me, and I was still beautiful.

Things got rocky when I had no friends to turn to. We were basically living in my house like an old couple with me sitting around at home while he went out and did things with the few buddies he had. At the beginning of grade ten he cheated on me, but I took him back because things were so confusing but he said he loved me so much and all he did was kiss another girl on the lips... and hold her hand at a concert. At this point my self- esteem dropped significantly because on the side, I didn't know why my scars were on my body because, hey, everyone picks so my scars CAN'T be from that.

To make a long and painful story cut short, the relationship ended at the end of grade eleven when he cheated on me with a girl who he admits is his true first love. A lot of unnecessary crap went down in the relationship that shouldn't have- one thing we never did was have intercourse. I've been single now for almost three years to the date and don't see myself with anyone anytime soon... if ever.

I remember on May 29th 2003, we were in the capital city of our province and he looked at me square in the eye and told me when I finally tried to break up with him, "*Angie, you are a freak. You know it, and no guy will ever want you*". As fucking sick and twisted as that manipulation tactic was, I took back my breakup statement and said we'd try things out... again. I knew what he said was true, and as horrible as it is now, I've only ever had that one relationship and I've lived up to that legacy now... three years later.

I have not dated because I cannot date. No guy could handle the emotional baggage, let alone the mental illnesses I face AND the physical scars they've caused. It's truly hideous and no one would be turned on after seeing such a deformed body. I see my life wasting away. Living your life knowing that you'll be alone is a sickening feeling that settles and burns in the pit of your stomach. We all deserve to love and be loved, but what happens when it'll never come your way?

This is one of the touchiest subjects concerning the whole picking situation. I do not want to be alone. I have alienated myself so far beyond reach now and I see my friends going from one relationship to another, most of them long term, and I stand on the sidelines just watching and offering third party advice. I'll never be able to gush to my friends about first kisses with boys. I need to keep myself distanced from males because the rejection would sting too much- the rejection of knowing that **I** am the reason why a guy can't date me. It's easy to say that there are nice guys out there who don't take appearances into consideration when looking for a mate, but what about the emotional instability I face? It's not even the sexual intimacy I desire, it's being held as I fall asleep in someone else's arms that I crave. Some days I am bitter and overly jealous of everyone who is relationship-capable... which happens to be everyone but me.

Of course no one understands if I have a crush on a guy why I cannot pursue it. It really does sound superficial and because it isn't, that means that something inside of ME is rotten. I can rant more about this, but I'm getting increasingly upset by writing this out. It's not therapeutic this time. It's exhausting and hopeless. I'm tired of living such an empty life knowing that I'll always be alone in this harsh world. Some days this is the reason why I don't want to get out of bed- to know that I'll never be able to start a family, to never know what it's like to be in love. A family of my own is all I ever really wanted... and it's my fault that goal can't be achieved.

That's it. This'll always be touchy, but hopefully proof to doubters that people who have Psychogenic Excoriation just can't "stop". It is an addiction and it has ruined me completely. This rant will keep going in circles and it's going to be hard to sleep tonight because I don't like thinking about this; writing it out and then *saying* these words is painful. No disorder should prevent someone from being able to be loved, but it does because I need to protect myself. I can't fall for someone, tell them these quirks about me little by little, and then face the rejection that I face from myself daily.

I definitely recognize that having a boyfriend won't cure everything, but I think I need acceptance and need to feel like someone cares about me more than platonically. I want to experience the glow in my eyes that my friends do when they speak of their significant others. I sink further into an abyss when I conclude: that person will never be me. Are these overwhelming emotions normal to have while getting some of this out for the first time? Is this a sign of healing or a deepening depression?

Real- Life Community   05-25-2006

My last day of being a teenager is being spent at the self-harm group, which is about an hour and a half bus ride away. I decided to go and I leave in one hour from now. Instead of spending my last day of childhood getting loaded or chilling with my friends, I'm entering adulthood with extra baggage and dealing with issues no one at any age should have to go through. This should be an enjoyable milestone in my life, but because of all the troubles I have I don't want to wait until I am an adult to start reversing the path of self- destruction. Though I decided to try and stop this compulsion far later than I should have (*it's taken me this long to recognize I had a problem*), at least I did make the decision to try anything to stop. Once you recognize that your quality of life is far worse than the "norm", it's hard to live with yourself because you know deep down that change needs to take place.

When I get there, what if I am going to be alienated because everyone there are cutters and don't recognize what I have as being self-harm... or even a problem?

Will I just sit there quietly and listen, or actually have the guts to tell "my story"? It's easy to do online but the words just don't come out the same face-to-face. The shame must actually be faced in the flesh instead of hidden away, masked by an electrical box.

Is this going to be a waste of my time? At least if it is, I won't kick myself over not going to the place or giving it a try. I'd always want to know if it was the key to some form of recovery had I not went. But I am leaving right now and am a **lot** more nervous than I expected.

There's No Holding Me Back   *05-26-2006*

So I went to the meeting yesterday, and it was the biggest waste of time ever. There was me, the two group coordinators, a social work student from my university who was observing, and another person seeking help. The meeting ran from 3:30- 5pm. I was hesitant about going because of my form of self-harm, but I felt welcomed. It was a *bit* shocking that no one had heard about Psychogenic Excoriation before, not even the social work student; she had heard about the condition before but never knew that there was a name for it. What made me feel, I guess more warmed to the situation, was when the women and the student became interested instead of thrown back by my condition that they wanted to learn more about it- and I wrote the name of the condition down for them. By them wanting to know, it shows that there are non-judgmental people still left in this incriminating world. Since they have taken their own struggles and used it to raise public awareness, they are inspirations. With workshops that they do, I feel that they are willing to research my condition and also inform people about this form of self-harm.

The most comfortable I felt was during the smoke break when I went out with the coordinators (because the other person there didn't say he really was a self-harmer- just had thoughts of it). We talked about our histories, some of it possibly influencing self- harming behaviors, yet it was casual and so natural to talk about it. It was almost as if it's desensitizing since we're all used to it at this point- the scars, the pain... and the knowledge of it becomes almost matter-of-factly and through this knowledge, it's easier to mature and not become emotional. Not to say that being emotional is a sign of immaturity, but usually a flow of unmanageable emotions come when we do not understand a situation (for example) - it's that involuntary ignorance from society that makes us suffer more. When you realize what's wrong, it's easier to compose yourself and speak about it... especially when you're driven for a positive change.

The most distinct detail of the meeting was when one of the ladies told me that we are normal, and that's the message that she wants people to realize. Initially it was hard for me to believe this- how is it normal to be your own worst enemy? But upon reflection, I'm thinking that we are all human, we all have our flaws, our own coping mechanisms, but it just so happens that self- harm is so shameful and it's the guilt of it that makes us feel so alienated. Because the scars are from ourselves and they are thought to be preventative. Maybe it's like any illness, but we weren't treated properly and we rely on self-harm as our survival technique. One woman said that being a self-harmer builds character within a person. Although it isn't the best way to define yourself as a person, you learn about the general pains that people face and you understand, as well as gain empathy, towards those who are less fortunate than yourself. I guess in order to get into the destructive pattern of being a cutter, you must face a lot of trials in life and this is the only satisfying way to cope with it for the moment.

It was briefly mentioned how I didn't get into the Acting Program, but we spoke about how there are other alternatives in how to achieve life goals. Then one of the women mentioned how she would love to someday have a script about self-harm put together and have people act it out with a film crew to show the world the realism behind these types of silent epidemics. That would be, for me, the most fulfilling life-goal to be able to do. Act, but tell a story about the trials and tribulations of humanity along with the personal struggles in life. How open these women are is what I want for myself, a recovered self-harmer who can spread words of hope and recovery to those who are still struggling. Maybe it will be me someday.

Today I'm 20 years old; now and for another 364 days. Third tanning session happens today at 1:15pm, from there I work from 2-8pm, and then it's time to try and celebrate my birthday with my family for a few hours.

I've been going through another depression. Depression always lingers in me but it's always a matter of how much control I have over it. A lot of things have been going on in my life recently and in order to hold on, I'm trying to think about good times just so I won't forget that I am capable of re-enacting them. I've been tempted to give up journaling about my skin- picking but somehow I find it therapeutic to just talk about it and everything that encompasses it because I want to figure it out.

Like during my "sessions" of picking was thinking to myself, "*What do you think of when you do this to your own skin?*" Maybe it's not as completely random as I've always thought because I think about stresses and what's currently bringing me down while doing it. I sometimes try to figure what caused the initial stress and my mind reverts back to past events which bring me down further. Then I realize that hours have passed because of my exhaustion from the concentration and dedication involved with picking.

Today I've been running to and from the bathroom/ computer for quick sessions on my face. While doing it I thought about how I have to go to my shit hole job in an hour and a half, along with the anxieties that have risen from being there. Tanning has been doing wonders except it hasn't done much for my upper arms or upper chest. My legs are clearing up significantly but of course with the massive amounts of scars on them, they'll never be normal/ scar-free or even remotely close to it. Since this is only a temporary fix to the problem I'm hoping that I'll get on a pill that will cut help reduce the OCD tendency to pick, come June 12th.

I Stand Alone   06-04-2006

Right now I'm feeling very disappointed in the after-effects of the tanning. I know I don't have an appropriate body image, but I actually thought that the colors of my skin were smoothing out. After I took self-portraits to compare to before, it looks as if the tanning has done nothing except what it's supposed to do to normal people: just make them darker.

I have hopes for a brighter future, but I just don't know how to get there. I keep hearing that there's no help for me and I have to fight this alone. I just can't- I don't know how. This journal has brought out emotions in me that have spooked me. One night after I wrote an entry here, I woke myself up in the middle of the night screaming... and I wasn't even having a nightmare.

I want to bring about awareness because I want change and help. Seeing the pictures from a 3rd person perspective have really dampened my mood, knowing that tanning isn't even masking the problem. Hell, I can't even stop this for **one. full. day**. Photographs are reminders that I'll always look horrid, even if I do magically get over the impulse/ compulsion part of this. I've fucked myself over and I feel like I ruined my life far before it, in theory, has even started.

With me starting to pick my arms these days, it feels like eventually I won't be able to leave the house... or if I do, I will have to in a snowsuit. Someone asked me the other day why I always wear the hood on my jacket and now that I think about it, it's the best way to hide myself; just wear my hood and sunglasses to stay hidden. I know I'm venting and I want hope, but after seeing the pictures and knowing that nothing has changed makes me think nothing will ever change. These constantly changing feelings of hope to helplessness are killing me- this emotional rollercoaster needs to make a stop somewhere.

I guess while thinking about mental illnesses, I'm ashamed and feel like I've brought this all on myself. Traits of Body Dysmorphic Disorder, BPD, and Depression... because they are learned behaviors, not purely biological like Bipolar is. So this could have been avoided years ago... if I knew that picking is fucking addictive and that I have an addictive personality, which is another fault in me, I would have never *touched* my skin. Or would I have? Probably. I'm susceptible to emotional pain, vulnerable to inner turmoil, which makes me feel so damned weak right now.

Some Days   06-08-2006

I'm glad that it is not the social fad to walk around in the nude. As liberating as general nudity is, to see someone exactly the way that he or she is born would mean that I am visibly the odd man out. Already I wear more clothing in this warm weather than other people due to my scars, so I would be wearing the same clothing now and everyone would actually wonder what I am hiding. With fashion being so important in creating *supposed individuality (*everything is already a copycat of something

52

else), it is more discreet that I am actually keeping secrets beneath my attire.

Lately my moods have not been great at all, so this brings on more of a tremendous guilt for picking. My life is only an addiction at this point- I'm a fucking empty vessel just living off of smokes and tearing my flesh apart. I plan on quitting smoking at the end of this pack now that I am jobless (I quit) and though it is difficult, it doesn't feel impossible like quitting picking. It's quite stupid of me, but I started smoking around last June during one of my deeper depressions because my twisted mind told me that in order to stop one addiction, you must pick up another one instead. And I hoped to stop picking and smoke instead because ***at least*** if I started smoking and quit picking somehow, there is help for quitting smoking: help lines, therapy, medications, support groups, etc. But with this compulsion, it's hard explaining to anyone how picking at your zits can turn into this... this vicious cycle that is more addictive than smoking. Reading my recent pack of cigarettes, it says that cigarettes are more addictive than heroine and cocaine. I don't know how much of that to believe but if that is so, then picking must be impossible to stop. How naive I can be, and now I'm stuck with two addictions. When I'm not partaking in one addiction, I'm doing the other.... or have it on the mind.

Here's to hoping that June 12th will begin to save me. My depression is yet again coming back- I think because I am unemployed. By being jobless all I'm doing is sitting around and dwelling on what I want to change, but can't. On June 12th I get new medications, probably an anti-psychotic since I've been on 7 different anti-depressants without positive results. Maybe they've gotten me out of bed mornings I wouldn't have otherwise, but I feel mentally sick. I want to inquire about a pill that my dermatologist wanted me on a year and a half ago when he crashed my world by giving me the ugly diagnosis of Psychogenic Excoriation. When the dermatologist sent me to my old-fashioned family GP, he told me that he would not put me on that drug because I'm not "crazy"- I do not have a crazed look in my eyes. As unprofessional and barbaric as that term is, he is right, I'm not crazy... even if I feel like it. This drug is supposed to reduce the need to pick your skin, but not stop it- some supposed form of therapy would be needed for that, therapy which is not offered around here.

Some days the bleakness of this whole scenario is overwhelming. And to know how it affects me: the ability to date, go to social events, it knocks me down a few notches. To know that essentially it's easy to "just stop" doing something no one else does, something that isn't even a substance, but for some reason... I can't, and I don't know why. What would I lose if I stopped? Absolutely nothing- my world would start turning around so I wonder why I keep torturing myself. I can't do anything but hate this, plain and simple.

Another Demolished Brick in the Wall   *06-09-2006*

The first real secluded summer I faced where I could not show my legs was the summer of grade nine going into grade ten. The summer of grade eight was when the addiction really got out of hand, but this story was about the next summer... I had just turned fifteen years old.

To make a long story short, I received a scholarship to a local entrepreneurship program that lasted one week. International students were there from Africa and Sweden, and it was a blast to get to know their lifestyles how much they differ from Canadians. We had different activities to do each day, and one of those days the activity was a long hike to the middle of nowhere to rock climb. While walking back to civilization at the end of the day, I tripped and fell on my left knee, which landed on a tree root. The pain was excruciating and it felt like I possibly dislocated my knee.

While sitting on the ground, the lady who was leading the group stayed behind a bit with me. Because of the injury, she asked me to lift up my pant leg. I absolutely refused to and she kept saying that she needed to see what kind of first aid was necessary for it. I kept saying that I'd limp back after a few minutes, but she then demanded to see my knee. I didn't want her to see the year of scars I put on my legs, scarring that I was still confused about (*until about one year ago*), but she said if I didn't lift up my pant leg she would cut my pant leg off because she was obligated to put her first aid to use. I was wearing my sister's sweatpants, so I had no choice unless I wanted to go home to an angry sister. Slowly I lifted my pant leg and made sure to put most of my left leg under her crouched body. This fight had gone on for about 10 minutes but it felt like it lasted a good hour.

She started looking at my knee and she then leaned back and saw my whole leg. The look of horror on her face is one I'll never forget, along with the gasp she made when she saw it. That's when I started bawling my eyes out; it wasn't because of the pain my knee was in, but from feeling like such a freak for looking the way I did (*do*). In a more frantic voice, she asked me if I was being abused at home and I quickly had to tell her that it was a skin disorder that was getting under control. It's strange when I look back now because that's the same excuse I use now to people the random times that they see it. I can't tell the truth to strangers, even if I speak candidly about it with my friends and family. It's not something that can be explained in a small paragraph with the expectation that it will be understood. At the time I didn't understand it, and to this day I still can't even explain it myself.

I limped back to the site we started at while holding onto her shoulder and another leader's shoulder, but I had to lie. By writing this out tonight I realize that I was being abused at home and still am- by myself. Her reaction, her face, it's what I'll have to deal with from people for the rest of my life.

Tattooed   *06-12-2006*

I'm feeling really selfish right about now. I ~~couldn't~~ didn't want to wait for the tattoo, though I've promised myself for months that I wouldn't get it until I have overcome this disorder. I don't want to make excuses or try to justify doing this, but my moods have been so erratic and I know that for the past 2+ weeks my anti-depressants have just stopped working. I've been less of a procrastinator, more apathetic, but am still picking my skin as much as before. Getting this tattoo was spontaneous, which I am far from... but it isn't completely spontaneous since I've been planning it for such a long time.

I'm disappointed that I didn't wait, but I am too overjoyed with the results to really care. Hopefully these are the wings that will help me through my journey, even if it does sound like true bullshit- I just need something to hold onto. With all of the significances these tattoos hold for me, I need motivation to keep fighting. The wings turned out so poetic in its art; hopefully it's more fuel to bring back some of my spark and somehow raise my self-esteem. Instead of the tattoos signifying achievement, it can signify struggling and overcoming... even if overcoming doesn't happen now: the fight to **never give up**. It feels like I won't overcome this disorder, that I will have to accept this as my life and make it as comfortable as possible. Like a person on a deathbed trying to make his last days as painless as possible, I'll have to do that for many years to come.

I was so nervous, but for the wrong reason. I was scared about having to take off my shirt in front of this stranger for her to be able to work on my back, but it wasn't about the fear of the needles driving into my skin. Hell, I self-injure, to put it bluntly, so what's the biggie about having someone else do it to me instead... but in a socially- accepted and artistic manner? The tattoo artist asked what the scars were from so she could know if I have complicated skin. Of course I told her it was acne scars... what other logical choice did I have for an answer? I bet if I told the truth she wouldn't understand plus she'd refuse to tattoo me since she'd assume I'd pick all the scabs off my tattoo and ruin it. You know, only a psycho would have a strange disorder like this. My sister wants me to wear tank tops now to show the tattoos off, but she's so naive to the shame I have for my scars and how I'd be subjecting myself to ridicule and questions about the scars. I won't deal with it unless it's absolutely necessary.

While sitting on the old- fashioned dentist's chair for a little over two hours half naked, my mind drifted until my eye caught a rising bump on my right arm. I stared at it intently hoping to rip it off my surface ASAP, but I had to cross my arms while sitting in the chair and grasp the armrests to make my skin tight. Then I thought about how wrong it was for me to want to get rid of something so natural on my body. I didn't remove it from my skin, but tonight I went to town on my eyebrows and have made myself satisfied with the results of the twisted addiction.

Right after the tattoo[s] I went outside and lit up a cigarette to relax. I still don't know which addiction to try and quit first and if I should completely overcome one before trying to attack another. My stash of cigarettes is becoming limited and I told myself I wouldn't buy any more, but I don't know if I should try to "*hit 2 birds with one stone*" or if I'll crash harder by doing that.

Finally, tomorrow is my psychiatrist appointment. I'm pretty sure that I'll be switched to an anti-psychotic from the current anti-depressant I'm on. I admit I am terrified with the results because it's a gamble to my well-being: he gives me the wrong one and I may actually lose my mind from off-balanced levels of chemicals, he gives me the right one and life becomes hunky- dory. I think the health professionals around here are convinced the right pill will stop addictions, but I'm not so convinced that there's a "miracle pill" to cure me. No one knows how to treat this, so I am confused about what needs to be done... but I don't feel the right steps are being taken, just the quickest ones for health "professionals" to get me out of their hair for awhile.

- CHAPTER II: The Day Treatment Program -

Where Do I Belong?   *06-16-2006*

*A*fter seeing the psychiatrists a few days ago, they both confirmed again that I have traits of Body Dysmorphic Disorder, but my main diagnosis is Borderline Personality Disorder. Instead of switching my meds to one that *could* work, they're going to gradually up my current drug to its maximum dosage. In grade twelve I was on a lower dose of this but then got placed another drug because this one made me feel numb. Not only did it wipe out sadness but I couldn't experience happiness. So again, I'll probably become zombie-like which doesn't please me because this pill doesn't even remove the feelings of depression. I expressed my concern with both psychiatrists in the room and the reason they're keeping me on it is because they want to rule out drugs one at a time by having dosages upped to the maximum. Here I go again feeling like the crazy guinea pig but I understand that I'll probably have to be on drugs for the rest of my life because every time I go off of them, I crash pretty quickly.

The woman psychiatrist asked me what I wanted to achieve by seeing them. I said that I want to stop picking my skin, want to find out why I started, and reduce the symptoms of my diagnosed disorders. She said that she doesn't know to what extent I pick my skin and she asked how I could explain the severity of it. All I did was lift my left pant leg and she said, "*Oh... now I know that you're serious about how bad it is*". Her reaction was kind of funny, in a warped sort of way. I have an appointment with the male psychiatrist next Monday to get more pills because he's calling them in week- by- week instead of giving them to me all at once (past suicide attempt, *cough*), but other than that I'm not quite sure why I have to see him so soon. They want to stick me in an emotions group or the 6 week "rehabilitation" day- treatment program which is in the capital city of my province. Then I got a call yesterday from someone who wants to give me a walk- around of the place on Wednesday to see if that's where I'd like to go. Fuck, I don't want to go, but I want to get better. So many things in my life will be discussed there that I'd rather forget even existed.

Both psychiatrists came to the conclusion that I pick my skin not only as a coping mechanism to things that have happened in the past, but because my OCD and anxiety is quite severe; no one has ever said that these symptoms were bad. I was told that anxiety occurs when I'm not releasing the tension in the usual ways that I do: smoking and picking. It's the anxiety that makes me continue the addictive patterns because with picking, I will do it until I feel fulfilled and satisfaction doesn't occur unless I get one good pick- whether it's when I start or hours in on a "session". But with the OCD, I've been told in the past to disregard that disorder as a primary diagnosis because picking is the only compulsive behavior I have that is uncontrolled. With my family history of OCD and how prominent this one compulsion is, my picking will be treated as if it's OCD because the same triggered "need" is constantly going off in the head. This is new information to me and I haven't viewed my disorder like this before. Hopefully it's a positive way to view it so change can come about, but I am terrified of this process of change- six long weeks, five days a week over in another city, just to straighten things out. My friend who just became a social worker told me he's heard that this program does wonders to people upon completion and it's basically the best method of mental health healing that this province has. I hope that this true and I'll be a new person come September when school gets in again... a person I don't ever remember truly being: happy.

I briefly mentioned this to friends, about this rehab... and I haven't received a single word of advice from anyone or any motivating feedback whatsoever. It saddens me how people get weird about serious topics, but we all have to face that just because most of us choose to not speak about the depressing truths in life, it doesn't mean they don't exist. Maybe with some people the darkness is more prominent, but I just feel more alienated and distanced from my friends... you know, with being twenty years old and needing rehab. This program specifically deals with emotions/ coping mechanisms but because there is individual therapy within this program, I'm assuming that I'll have cognitive therapy and have to work **harder** than I ever have to beat this. Thinking about it makes me want to give up without trying, but I have to do everything I can because this is my last resort.

A few days ago, I found out that Bobby's dad died after a long battle with lung cancer. Since we currently aren't friends, I called his best friend to ask if I should call him and send my condolences since I knew he'd be a wreck. His friend immediately told me calling wouldn't be a good thing because his father's death hit him hard. I didn't know exactly what that meant until yesterday morning when I read someone's blog and found out that Bobby ODed on the last of his father's medications. He has been in the ICU now for 3 days and is slowly waking up from his coma but no one knows yet if there's any brain damage because he has only mumbled 10 words in 2 hours.

When I found out what happened yesterday, I called the local hospital to see if he was there and he was so my sister and I booted it down there. Of course his family wasn't there visiting and I found out from his best friend that there were about 10 people at his house who didn't call the ambulance when they saw him passed out on the couch and turning blue... for 3 hours. At the hospital, his best friend Anthony and Anthony's mom have been alternating with visiting him; both today and yesterday his family wasn't there to visit him and that was my #1 fear... that no one would be there for him. Anyway, yesterday I lied to get into the ICU saying that I was a cousin from out of town and when I saw him in the room... I lost it. Respirator, charcoal coming out of his mouth, heart monitors, tubes...

His yellowed eyes opened once in a while but then rolled in the back of his head; I think he got one look at me. I didn't want him to see me because I don't know if I'm a trigger right now to him or if he'd really

62

want me there, so I hid behind Anthony's mom. What really upsets me is that the night he supposedly did this, my cell phone was ringing off the hook early in the morning but I didn't answer it because I was in a kerfuffle with another friend and I didn't want to chance it being him. After narrowing it down, to people telling me it wasn't them calling... I think it was Bobby. I know he called someone else too, a person who also didn't pick up her phone. He was so alone and he knows I'm there when he needs it.... actually, maybe he didn't know...

I've been in the same position, but not as close to death as him. I can relate so much to the pain, but I've never had to watch someone else go through this alone- someone who has shared my bed and someone I've had such an erratic relationship with. I've never stopped caring for him, although the romantic feelings have been long gone. I've watched his life spiral downhill from being in a relationship with him, to being his friend, and then watching from afar.

I'm still going to kick his ass WHEN he gets out (I won't accept that he's not)... even if I already know what it's like to feel like there's nothing else to live for. Kicking his ass in the sympathetic way of course, but I didn't think this reaction would happen so quickly after his father's passing. I'm not going to see him until he's awake and able to comprehend more and tell Anthony whether or not he wants to see my family or me. Anthony will ask him and he'll make the choice, but he'll most likely kick my ass for seeing him in a coma… but I'll deal with him later on with that one.

I really want to see him and talk to him. Since he was being a prick when we were friends I feel so gullible for jumping back in his life, but I know he's just so damned sick. I'm hoping he'll be forced into some sort of counseling to grieve over his father's death. After being in his life for so long, I know how to handle him but when my health is down it's hard to deal with bullshit. Right now none of that matters because he needs to know that he still has people around who love him and are looking out for his best interests. I could have contributed to his feeling of loneliness by not being there until he had already done the deed. I could be too late in letting him know...

I'm now being redundant by writing far too much but my emotions are in complete turmoil. What's a positive though is that through this pain I'm feeling, I know what it's like to be on the receiving end of suicide- the friend left over to pick up the pieces. Even in a time of need I feel like I can always have someone to turn to, even if my perception is clouded; I have more than Bobby thinks he does and never want to put my friends/ family through my attempt again.

It's Been Awhile   06-30-2006

Much has happened in these past two weeks which has forced me to put my writings aside. Bobby is now living with Anthony and has suffered no brain or organ damage, thank God. I am now in the 6 week day treatment program and have just completed my first week.

In terms of skin picking, I'm still confused about how this program will benefit me; will it help me to calm my overall general anxieties and to reduce my obsessive-compulsive tendencies? We were told in one of the "classes" to create goals that we want to accomplish for the week. One of mine, without going into extreme detail with the class, was to reduce my picking sessions to 10 minutes at the max. The problem with this is I've made introverted excuses to sneak to the bathroom more frequently (*maybe an hour after a session*) and do it again for another 10 minutes. So maybe it's more sessions, but at least I have more awareness.

Yesterday's classes were more intense than I expected and I ended up picking for a long time afterward, so maybe I should speak to my case coordinator about what the best way to stop/ reduce is, or maybe that will come as I'm given the proper "tools" to cope with life. Maybe right now and for the next two weeks, I'm not ready.

Screaming for Air   07-02-2006

About a week ago, I went to visit my ex- boyfriend at the hospital. When I arrived, Anthony's mother was there. She is a former nurse who dealt with burn victims years ago. I said hi to her, a sweet woman who means well, and she asked me if I went south this summer because of my tan. I told her I didn't, so she immediately knew that I have been going tanning since there are no other options (financially) to get skin darker... and the sun hasn't been out enough this summer for any pigment changes. She looked at me sympathetically and asked why I am destroying my body. She then explained to me that tanning is as dangerous as smoking is to the body and that I'm slowly killing myself. She doesn't know I smoke, so I snickered on the inside about the coincidence, but she said that there may be a day where I'm in the hospital because of what I do. I was agreeing with her, but it was for different reasons.

The whole time I kept my mouth shut because I couldn't think of an excuse, a lie, and I'm tired of conjuring up ideas to justify what I do. Of course this disorder isn't known to people, but they should get some sort of hint that I don't do it just to get darker/ be "sexier" since I don't dress to impress... anyone. When she left, I flopped at the end of my ex's bed and we chatted about many things for a while. We haven't spoken about my disorder, not even a whole lot when we became friends a year after the breakup. But with his fragile state I decided to open up a bit more to him- he's the only male I've been with sexually for a long period of time and it started 6 years ago and ended 3 years ago, so he knows about my disorder; he was in my life just before the picking got out of control.. We have since moved on romantically and have been friends; we know we will always have each other's backs because we're like brother and sister. Here's a synopsis of our conversation:

Me: You know why I go tanning.
Him: The scars?
Me: Yeah. It helps a bit, but not a lot.
Him: (*looks off and pauses*) I couldn't imagine living everyday with what you have. It must be so hard, and so many years later too...

He looked so sad and empathetic about it. I haven't seen him show that sort of emotion toward my disorder ever. A long while back he used to get angry with me for picking my skin while watching TV and even said I was picking at non- existent imperfections. It was different that he sounded so sad and was so open with me about his feelings... it was a nice change. He sounded like he understood, not the situation, but the pain involved and he was able to somehow relate.

With the program I'm in for the next five weeks, I was talking to a person I met online the other night and he told me he can relate to the pain as well. I never would have guessed, but you can never predict the pain someone is in or what they are thinking.

I have to write an introduction letter about why I am in this program and then present it to the group on Thursday. Much of it will have to do with this aspect of my life along with the possible underlying reasons as to why I do it. I keep trying to write it and now it's near completion but I keep getting upset, more ashamed, and then cross out a lot of emotion linked to the words. I don't want to cry in front of people, even if they have cried in front of me. It must be that "*I have to be strong*" front I've always had that's making me worried about not holding back the tears.

We're Always in Repair   *07-05-2006*

The other day I went out for my smoke wearing a jacket with the hood up and my big brown sunglasses. My sister and her boyfriend were outside and he looked at me and said, "*God, you look like [a celebrity who is known for her drug use and big sunglasses]*". It pissed me off and I think I just kind of grunted back at him just because I'm not in the mood to get into it with people anymore. It's not that I think Nicole Ritchie is revolting, but I know that her name is used as a criticism because of her Hollywood status and there are rumors surrounding her lifestyle.

Since my sister is quite open about her own issues, she took it upon herself to tell her boyfriend about my skin picking. I forget what excuse she used to say she "needed" to tell him, but I'm not happy because it's no one's business except for who I choose to tell... or am forced to tell. She also found "a reason" to tell him other things about me too, but she just doesn't know where to draw the line. Even if I'm in the washroom for more than an hour while he's here, I'd rather someone tell him I'm masturbating or something...

Today was my last day of tanning. It reduces the scars minimally, but not enough for me to continue to fry my skin to death. Ruining my skin to cover up mutilation doesn't sound logical to begin with. Tomorrow in class I get to read my introduction letter about why I'm in the day treatment program. It's an angsty letter with thoughts in there I've never actually expressed out loud to anyone.

Awake, but Still I'm Dreaming   07-06-2006

Today I finally met someone who suffers with the same obsession I do. I met her in group; she has the "sister syndrome" of Dermatillomania called Trichotillomania (Trich). It's comforting to actually see with my own eyes that I am not alone... even though I don't wish this on anyone.

This woman is in her first week of group and I'm in my second now, so today I had to read an introduction letter which involved a lot of talk about this disorder. Not only did I read the letter but I was wearing a jean dress which showed my shoulders, a bit of my upper chest, half of my back, and about four inches above the knee. I wanted everyone to see that I'm not just a whiney child who over-exaggerates her flaws for attention, but that this is something that has destroyed my inner and outer self. In a sick way, I was hoping that all of these remarkable people who I've known in this short time would distance themselves away from me... just so that I don't get any closer to them before they find out about my deformities. But they respect me more for doing it, and say that I'm brave. I didn't cry while reading my letter though my voice trembled as much as my hands did- but I almost lost it while describing my fears about my near-rape scenario.

I heard feedback from the group; a few of the men said that when they met me that they thought I was an attractive young woman. It took a bit of restraint to bite my lip because when we are given a compliment we are being trained to say "Thank you", and not "Thank you, *but*". While these comments angered me, one comment really stung me when another woman told me that the scars are not that bad but I know that somehow she was sugar-coating the truth because of what I had done to expose myself. I felt naked while wearing that dress, an outfit that many people wear daily.

The first woman came up to me after that class session and showed me her "wounds" from Trich. I couldn't help but immediately feel for her just because of how consuming having an impulse control disorder is. She has a bald spot on her head, but only a few scars on her body that are barely noticeable. So her picking is minimal but the Trich is out of control. For me, the Trich is minimal but the amount of skin-picking is obviously absurd. She thanked me for telling "my story" and she was too embarrassed to comment during the question period in front of the group, which is why she brought me aside. It's gestures like this that make me feel somewhat influential and somehow validated for the pain I've gone through... that I opened up someone else and made her feel more comfortable in this sometimes intimidating group therapy.

In the group I found more common links with a guy a bit older than me- his name is Tony. Though he doesn't pick his skin we found indirect thoughts about the disorder and much in common when it comes to feelings. He drove me home and we ended up talking in his car for hours straight. Wow.

Today has been an eye opener in many ways and I'm hoping that it's a positive thing- to find things in common with people, to not feel so alienated. It definitely brings a new light to life and hope that there is a safe haven out there to emotionally free your true self without judgment, and to have a great support system. For the first time in my life I feel like I can be myself, have my faults, that I'm worthy of meeting such inspirational people, and am deserving of having this safety net. This is the best thing I've ever done for myself and I couldn't have picked better timing in my life than now to be able to meet the people I have- and I'm only in my second week, with four more to go.

It Hurts to Believe   *07-15-2006*

I don't know if things are getting better with therapy, generally speaking. I know it has not affected my skin- picking at all. My case coordinator told me on the first day that I won't stop picking, but hopefully if I'm given tools to manage my stress/ anxiety, my picking will reduce. I'm starting my 4th week of 6 and everything feels hopeless right now. The professionals have been doing everything they can to make me cry and it's been isolating to know that I don't bawl my eyes out like everyone else. I'm only realizing now what people mean when they've been telling me for years that I'm emotionally detached. It's a fucking awful feeling. All of these feelings are now coming out, but they're coming out at such a fast rate that I feel like I'm not in control of myself anymore... even though I knew I was never truly in control to begin with.

I don't know if it was just because I was having a bad day when I went to the program on Monday or Tuesday, but I decided to wear the outfit that I was given for my dance performance a few months ago (which I didn't attend because it showed the scars on my upper body). I was feeling crappy after given humiliating feedback about not feeling emotions, and I went to the washroom. I glimpsed in the mirror and felt even more embarrassed about daring to wear that spaghetti- strapped tank top. The scars on my arms have multiplied significantly and I didn't even realize it until that day.

There's more to write, but I just can't right now. Everything just seems to be spinning and I just can't tell if it's steering in the right direction or spiraling out of control.

I flipped out and vented to my fellow programmers today in the cafeteria and feel stupid for it. Let out a lot of angst/ frustration about my life and then went into specifics with how skin picking has ruined it. How I can't get a boyfriend/ husband, have a family, go to a public beach, wear summer clothes, etc. Afterward, they told me that I didn't flip out at all but because I don't express these thoughts, it felt like I was selfishly taking centre stage.

Today I had an appointment with my case coordinator and temporary arrogant asshole psychiatrist. My pill is now upped from 225mg- 300mg. They may put me on a mood stabilizer too, one for people with bipolar even though I've never had a manic episode- my life is a continuous depressive state and they are well aware of that. They're treating my condition solely as OCD and doping me up to hopefully reduce the need to pick my skin, but how can something I've done my whole life just magically disappear with pills? That's just dreaming of candy canes and lollipops.

This program can't help me stop, so I wonder why I'm here. I'll never be able to stop picking and I've already damaged my body, along with my mind. It's easy to hide scars of the mind, but not so much the physical scars of the body. Both are permanent and harmful, but one can be hidden while the other is a physical reminder is always there to cause heartache.

The experiment of documenting my struggles with this shitty disorder was also a way of seeing if I can avoid habits and patterns. I've identified more recently, but it just makes it more frustrating to recognize patterns but not know how to change them. Simply, I could just not raise my hands to my skin and the scars would heal, plus I wouldn't be creating new wounds. Unfortunately, it's not that easy and I remain trapped in my own prison of never-ending vicious cycles. It's getting worse, slowly but surely.

It really does feel like I'm trapped and there's no solution or cure. Nothing to reduce the picking and in a few years from now, I can see myself completely covered with scars. How can a person live like that? I want to turn things around and I've tried so damned hard without any success; I've just had further disappointments and failures. It feels like I've ruined many things in my life, things that humans are entitled to- and I have now permanently missed out on future opportunities of happiness. It's harder to accept that I've fucked up my life completely and people are saying I'm just being too hard on myself, but I don't know what to do anymore. It's stupid to keep this journal. I'm saying this now because I'm fed up and frustrated with what I've ultimately done to myself. Not only for the years I've missed out on, but for the years that I'll have to watch pass me by.

None of this is fair. The day treatment program has ruined me. I've sunk into a serious depression filled with more self-hate, guilt, and self-blame... maybe ever. I don't know where my life is going but I know I have to adjust to the fact that there's no cure, no one has answers, and

73

no one cares to find out how to fix this. I can't fix this. I need help that isn't available. This all seems pointless.

I'll Give Anything, Except Give Up   07-31-2006

I'm out of my slump for the most part, once I gave a week for my new dosage of meds to kick in. With the day treatment program, I'm in my 5th week of 6, but I'm going for a 7th week part time. I was confronted today by the resident psychiatrist after the first class of the morning called "Feelings Group". In feelings group, I stated that I was disappointed in my progress because of how I came here to find tools to stop my picking.

So he comes into the lounge where I was flopping on the couch, alone and being anti- social, and tells me that he and the other psychiatrist were talking about me. They said that since it's my second last week, they want to put me on a **behavioral intervention**. Yep. I have to quit cold turkey for the umpteenth time, but the difference this time is that I have support from the group. Upon reflection, I recognize that a reason why I keep going back to it (*other than the addictive nature of it*) is because a flow of uncontrolled emotions come gushing out when I stop picking. For the five full weeks I've been here, they've been trying to get emotion out of me which is hard so now there will be two supposed benefits. They want me to cry which isn't something I do often, but I'll probably cry now. On the bus ride home I touched my face and was about to pick off a scab but noticed, so I held onto my Discman for dear life the rest of the ride home. By tomorrow morning I know I'll be an emotional wreck. The sign will be going back up on the mirror tonight to block my reflection and I'll pre-occupy myself by playing video games and by not being in the bathroom long at all.

I'm terrified. I don't want to be emotionally unstable by doing this because the urges will be too strong- without acting them out, the anxiety will come out emotionally. I have also come to the conclusion through this program of how alone I am in the real world. This fact has been pounding at me because I have no one to go to for support. I don't even want to tell my immediate family about this intervention to chance a slightly negative comment such as, "*Well you've tried to stop before so what's so different now?*" I'm feeling so alone, terrified, alienated, and I basically slept my weekend away. My friends aren't the best support right now for this whole process of me being in an emotional rehab and they have been nagging at me to hang out when I tell them I'm not in a socializing mood.

No one understands any of this, no one is here, and the safety net of this program will be gone in two weeks. Even if I DO manage to stop for two weeks, what will happen when I get thrown back into my shit hole life? I'll be the same, and still detached from my peers. This is it for me- this is the only safe place I have to go crazy from "withdrawals" at. If I don't try my hardest now, I'll never have the opportunity to try again.

This is my last attempt at recovery. Well, I would like to say it'll be the last time I'll try because if I fail, I don't want to continue on living like this. That damn drive inside of me, the self- destructive and torturous one, won't let me quit even if I fail this time. I think it's because I must sadistically strive on failures; this place is the best place to stop at.

I'm going to see if I can find any crappy ole' fake nails around the house to make it more obvious/ conscious to myself that I am trying to pick.

Why the fuck is all of this so hard? I need motivation, but how can I find it when I feel so damn alone?

Far Away For Far Too Long   *08-01-2006*

Yesterday I ended up picking only 7 scabs. So much for no scabs at all but it's near impossible while in the shower. This morning I picked at two and am now typing away to try and fight this. I really wanted to quit cold turkey, so it feels like I failed myself. I know deep down that I haven't, that this is the start of something long-term... but not attaining my goal like planned makes me feel even more weak and powerless. It's as if I'm a victim of myself. I kept dreaming about this whole situation last night and now it feels as if I didn't get an ounce of sleep, like a truck hit me and dragged my mutilated carcass for miles along the side of the road. I'm going to the program today but I can't see how I can possibly stay awake for the entire day.

I was extremely bitchy toward the family because of my abnormally high levels of anxiety. There is a constant tingling underneath my skin and I can't stop trembling. I couldn't find the glue to the fake nails, so that idea is canned. The key to all of this is to not look at myself at all- in the mirror or down on my skin. It's nearly impossible to not glance down at yourself, so there's where my slip ups have been- during my moments of weakness where I almost force myself to look, just to torture myself, to fight the urges... which I cannot do 100%. It pisses me off that something is so powerful and consumes my self- worth; I've bowed down to this disorder for too many years now. When I find my eyes scanning or my hands roaming to find imperfections, I've been either grabbing onto something tightly or I look up at the ceiling for a few seconds. It doesn't get rid of the anxiety; this self- discipline is truly torturing me while draining me of energy because I have to focus intensely just to move on to the next minute without mutilation.

I told my family about it without any derogatory comments, but when I felt the urges come on strongly and had nothing to do, I begged my mom for the Internet and she snapped at me saying she also had stuff to do online. I tried to explain to her that I needed something immediately to do to completely take my mind off the urges. My sister was playing with the video games, so Mom got mad saying that she had been waiting to go online and to stop bugging her. She did give it to me about 10 minutes later but told me to never whine like that again or she'll take the password off of the Internet and I'll never go on again.

Again, I feel so alone. Even while writing this entry I felt the need to touch my face, to feel a slight scab, but I had to refrain from picking it off. This is taking way too much effort that I don't know I actually have and don't think it's humanly possible to have. I think it's the alienation that's eating me up the most about this; I am truly fighting this alone. The program people will be more than supportive but at the end of the day I'm left to deal with me. And I hate things that I don't understand. How did I actually acquire this rare disorder? Why can't the little tick in my brain just stop so I can learn to live again? Will the tick be this strong for the rest of my life where I'm fighting each minute not to pick? If so, it's impossible to do this. I've already ruined 1/3 of my life; the age of 26 isn't too far away and by then I'll have ruined precisely half of my life if I continue on like this.

To Rewrite My Ending   08-04-2006

It's exhausting to repeatedly force your brain to tell your hands to not do something that they are so used to doing, along with not looking at yourself or rubbing parts of your skin to see if there is something to remove. When I feel or see an abnormality on my skin my initial reaction is to remove it- it doesn't belong there and though I know logically that I'm making the problem worse by creating redness/ inflammation/ scabs, something sordid inside of my brain feels that I'm doing myself some sort of favor.

I was ready to blow the other day when the psychiatrist told me that they all underestimated the severity of my disorder, so they wasted five weeks trying to force out emotions that are impossible to feel at this time. They thought that my behavior would reverse if I got feelings out but the psychiatrist realized that this is my roadblock to feeling anything. It's true because in the last few days I have been a chaotic mess and feel like I'm going insane! Every emotion is intensified because of the anxiety I'm drowning in. I expressed to them how it feels like I have lost a part of me, even how it feels as if I've lost everything because I feel out of control with how damn hard I have to fight the urges. I know I'm gaining control by stopping myself but this really takes up a large portion of my life- trying to stop takes up ALL of my mental energy and conscious thoughts. I told the psychiatrist that I was taken back at how no one in

78

the program took this seriously until my 6th week of the 6 week program and she said she appreciated my assertiveness to tell her about my dissatisfaction. Now, I will be going part time next week... AND the week after because everyone feels as if I'm just starting the program now in terms of potentially reaching my feelings.

A problem that leads me to picking is how I disassociate my mind from my body. I didn't realize it before but when I speak about my body, I refer to my body as "it", not "me". The only thing I consider to be "me" is my mind- the logic, intellect, and rationality. Because of this I had to write a letter from my mind to my skin and read it out loud in group so that I can find the connection, within my myself, to feel that I am my body. Now I have to write a response from my skin to my mind. It sounds a little hokey and I'm not too sure it will turn out anything more than a fascinating fable.

My body is aching from trembling so much. My mind isn't functioning up to par because I'm feeling so lost, confused, and alone. I've been having nightmares, when I actually do sleep, about slow torture that leads to death. Not everyone believes in dream analyses but I believe, and my shrink said it too, that it's happening because I have to put myself through torture daily just to get by. She also said that this living minute-to-minute struggle will last a few months, but I seriously don't know if I can take months of this. But I have no choice ultimately... it's this or my life. On the positive side of things, my face has cleared up nearly 100%; there is *only* one half opened wound I know I ripped open the night before last while in a semi- conscious state. I've never in my life seen my face so clear; my upper chest is the same now but my shoulders are still recovering. My legs on the other hand have barely shown progress which is frustrating and makes me unsure that stopping this habit is worth it. I do know that skin cells shed much more frequently on the face and upper chest than any other body part.

This is the hardest thing I've ever done and I hate feeling so isolated in this, unable to reach out for support when I need it the most.

How Long 'Til This Aching Disappears?   08-06-2006

I hate the phrase "live for the moment". If I followed that, I'd be right in the bathroom this moment not caring about the damage I'd be inflicting on my skin. This morning I had a triggering event that upset me so in I went again. I only did it for about 2 minutes, but I'm not supposed to do it at all. I still have not went a single day completely pick-free; this past week I've picked at maybe a few in a day, adding up to about 2 minutes. It's still disappointing since I'm not reaching my goal, even if the results have been more visible.

I tried explaining my "detox" to a close friend the other day and it was virtually brushed off. Well, more not acknowledged as anything severe... or even a real issue. This makes me feel more alone and I realize that I do not have support around here. Only one person outside of my immediate family moment is being a support but sometimes goes about it the wrong way- my ex, Bobby. It still helps that I do have friends here because there is empathy/ understanding and an attempt to help; that attempt in itself is a relief because it shows that someone cares. Another friend I have is away at the moment but I don't want to burden him with this since he's been there for me for a lot of the hard shit already. Hell, I don't want to bother anyone with this pain because if someone connects with me they will know the pain and no one should be able to relate to this. I've been wearing my usual frumpy clothes but this time for a different reason. Before it was to hide my shame/ scars from the world but now it's also to hide from myself so that I cannot see my flesh. If I do, then I get "triggered", and trying to fight the trigger is too damn hard.

Socially, I want to do something drastic or mean, just so that everyone will actually hate me and leave me alone. It sounds screwy but right now that is my thought. Of course I'm not going to but I wish that everyone would go away because, in a way, I am alone but fighting loneliness while having people around is even harder than being completely isolated with no one around. I don't know if that makes any sense; the idea that the loneliness I face is purely emotional, from the lack of solid connections I have with people.

I've been online but am not bothering to talk to people these last few days or if so, only minimally. I just can't express myself and when I do it's either that I'm doing incorrectly, which doesn't get my point across, or the person just isn't capable of understanding. How do I expect someone to get it when it's confusing as hell to me? I just can't deal with people lately, even the few understanding people, because I've just been a mope and everyday it's the same ole' shit story, just a new day. I don't want to drag people down with me. I have homework to do over this long weekend and I should get started on the relapse prevention sheets (*LOTS of them*) but right now I don't know what good it will do when I still haven't gone a whole day without picking. Yesterday I had a better day but these mood shifts are killing me because every emotional fall I have becomes deeper and my need to be away from people grows stronger. When will things start looking up?

Another Ditch, You Keep Moving   08-12-2006

I stopped the intervention the day before yesterday due to one of the most hopeless depressions I've had yet. I can't even fake being ok anymore, like I could with other depressions. I have no real immediate future when it comes to hopes, goals, or desires. The resident psychiatrist said I put myself into this slump by abruptly stopping the picking. Well fuck you because that's what I was SUPPOSED to do, so don't you dare put the blame on me.

They want me back in the program for a 9th week out of 6, and possibly a 10th. I'm just tired of it all. I've been stripped of everything that I was even remotely satisfied with about myself and am left here exposed with no where to hide, no where to go.

How Do I Go Forward?   08-13-2006

Despite the intervention being a flop, I learned a lot about my physical self and my emotional self. Not everything I learned was positive, but I was able to start reversing some of my thoughts that I assumed were forever embedded in my head. It really felt like a new start, with such a great support system at the hospital... but I needed more than that. People who are associated with me in the real world were less than caring, as they have been throughout this whole rehabilitation process but it really sunk in for me last week. Maybe it's because this is the only time ever I've openly admitted that I need social support in order for this to be a success. It pisses me off that I need some sort of support from people, as if it's a form of validation because I went a few days stressing about how I felt non-existent.

Though I went through the shakes, the daily minute-to-minute struggles for **a week and a half,** no the lack of sleep, the strong stench of loneliness that is still overwhelming, bursts of emotions, etc, I did have progress that I cannot and REFUSE to deny. I may have crashed in this pursuit and currently have no fucking motivation to try again, but there are things that I've learned about myself that won't disappear with this trial:

PHYSICALLY:

1.   I saw a face for the first time. I wasn't supposed to, but I couldn't help but touch my face spontaneously and love my newfound smooth texture.

2.   This is the strangest part of it, but I noticed that I actually have womanly curves on my upper body. Once the wounds healed it's as if I could see past the mutilation and see a grown woman. I felt my age, instead of a pre-teen.

3.   I wanted to wear makeup. I wasn't allowed to look in the mirror to put it on, even though I must admit I had to take sneak peaks from far away to view my progress. I didn't want to wear it to hide something, but

like a little girl mimicking her mother, I wanted to wear it to see if I could go that extra step and see myself as being pretty.

4.   My stomach is completely healed and even now I don't have a desire to "search" for any abnormalities. Hopefully this is a lasting accomplishment. The tops of my shoulders are still somewhat smooth and I hope to keep it that way, but who knows?

EMOTIONALLY:

1.   It was the hardest thing I've ever done in my life and though it was only for a week and a half, which was 110% pure torture, I managed. I am dedicated and still motivated to succeed, even if it currently feels hopeless... I don't want to give up.

2.   I'm not the loveable and fun-loving Angie that I created to hide my disorder and pain. I may have those qualities but I have no choice but to recognize how gloomy I really am.

3.   Surprisingly, I'm a highly sensitive person who fears rejection/ hurt/ pain/ confrontation and doesn't take it lightly when it occurs. By suppressing my emotions in the past I pretended that things didn't bother me, but I have to deal with the fact that the reason I suppressed everything is because pain is overwhelming for me. It's as if I feel emotions deeper than the average person, so I shut out emotion over the years to not have to feel the negative ones anymore. Unfortunately, that meant that I lost the ability to ever feeling happiness as well.

Last night I really wanted to die. I hate these cycles of depression because with every fall comes a deeper sense of hopelessness because it's reinforcement that my dark side is correct about my self- worth. While lying down in my bed, I wondered how many other people who have a life-consuming and unspoken disorder for as long as I have are actually still alive. Sure I've tried to off myself before, but what **is** keeping me here now? No matter how much of myself I lose, there will always be that fighter side of me because I've always hated the idea of giving up. Giving up hope and life is equivalent to admitting my powerlessness, whether it's imaginary or real. My head just kept doing circles about the best suicide method and how to sharpen it up from my previous attempt. I didn't want to attempt it last night, but thinking about it was soothing- to dream about not feeling like this anymore. This morning I felt somewhat refreshed when I woke up; still down about all the same things, but my mood had changed. I hope I can maintain one mood through all of this shit so I can stay in control because there may come a time again where I'm not in control. The program wants me to "feel" emotions, but now I remember why I avoided feeling them- because of how hopeless it is to feel, and it hurts too much.

Since my day was a very bleak one, a friend came over to visit and cheer me up. He ended up getting snippy because he was losing a game against my sister, so I went back into my funk and I lied down on my bed because I couldn't take it. Tonight has been the first night that he hasn't called me to see how I've been doing, which he's been sweet to do every night, but I know he isn't pissed at me. He's probably taken back by my reaction to his bitchiness which I usually handle by getting him in a good mood again, but I this time I just shut down. Seeing that my friends are dropping like flies, whether or not they were real to begin with, I'm not exactly doing a good job of keeping people around.

I'm still frustrated that I have to go for my 8th week starting tomorrow and it will be extremely hurtful saying goodbye to all the people who have been in the program with me since day one. I should be well enough to graduate too, not be worse than I started off. But am I really worse or am I now allowing myself to see what kind of fucking shitty and pretentious life I created? I tried hard to better myself in the past and thought I was on the right track mentally (not concerning my disorder) because I created a life that I really wanted to have... but I just couldn't keep up with the demands it had. This is the chance to finally be me. I know who I am and who I've always been, even though I lost sight of it and yearned to reverse the miserable traits that consume me. This misery gives me crucial insight to other people's suffering and gives me the cursed gift of empathizing with others.

I hated the possibly of being seen as the whiny kid because in junior high I was starting to be seen like that, so I changed around my persona for high school and everyone loved me! I kept it up to make others around me happy and hoped I'd become that person because I had some of those positive traits in me. I took pride in these past five years as being seen as strong and independent; I didn't talk about the concept of relationships when it came to myself, and people admired that in me because I was able to prove that I didn't need someone by my side in order to shape who I am and I also didn't need to ask for help from anyone. I'm not as strong as I'd like to be and unfortunately I'm not the emotionless and robotic independent woman I thought I was. I am capable of having feelings that make me feel weak and I now find myself seeking guidance.

For tomorrow morning, I must write some unspecified work about why I feel powerless. They are assuming that if I tackle that emotion for THIS week, that I'll be aaaalll better for the next one. How do I rid of that feeling when I can't control urges to self-harm, have feelings that will hurt others I certainly don't want to, feel powerless to stop this addiction, and now feel powerless about going to school/ work/ finding finances when I've always been the one to do both and be successful? So many other "issues" of powerlessness are ruling my life but every time I write about a fucking feeling, it intensifies, which is why I am useless. No one is hearing me and I have to scream to tell them; instead of listening to what I say, they just dodge questions and ask, "*How do you feel about that?*" It's discouraging that I'm on a time constraint to get well with September coming around the corner- I must either work or go to school, but I cannot function without picking my skin. The professionals know it and aren't willing to help me with that concern. They know that even if I go through another intervention, I'll be destined to fail. I need to function and succeed instead of wasting money on university with getting shitty marks OR be absent-minded at a job and get fired.

My friend just called; we know that we have to mature our friendship since we both act like brats around each other (probably because we met as kids), but we're both going through rough times and need each other's friendship more than ever. All I can hope in every situation is that honesty will strengthen my friendships because now I've got a reason to filter out the pawns in my life. They weren't there for me when I needed it and **now** is when I need it.

Three days ago, my depression was a little more than out of control. Now I'm starting to be able to analyze things both for the pros and cons without having emotions overrule my logic. When I let feelings get the best of me, the negative ones always win. That is another explanation about why I suppressed emotions for many years; I have lost control and have been embarrassed by my own irrationality, which is what I've been experiencing lately.

I took pictures of myself today but there has definitely been a new change while taking them; I am even more self-conscious of the results. Why? Through this intervention I have felt this "connection" that I was told I needed to feel, to connect my body and mind into one entity. Now I feel more exposed- before I wouldn't show people I know the pictures because I was ashamed but now it's because I'm really feeling self-conscious. By connecting my mind with my body and feeling sporadic emotions daily, I think I have lost the ability to act onstage. I can no longer put myself in someone else's body momentarily in order to forget that it is my body in front of an audience.

I just finished looking at the last batch of pictures that were taken and I'm shocked at how well my upper chest, arms, and even my face are doing. My legs looked like they were doing better before but I was also frying my skin under the lights. By comparing my pictures, being more than two months apart in date, it gives me more of a motivation to want to go through an intervention again. But I can't do that if I'm being thrown back into school or work and it's very upsetting that I have no choice but pick at my skin in order to function, which is what I'll have to do for work and school.

It's Been a Lifetime   08-16-2006

Somewhat unexpectedly, it was announced today that I'm saying my goodbye to the program tomorrow. I knew that it was approaching quickly and I've only stayed these extra few weeks to try out a new lifestyle and to hold onto what seems to be the only hope left for my life. As of Saturday, I will not have that safety net to go to on days that I don't feel that it is best to be alone. One fear I have now is that I'm more vulnerable to ridicule since I cannot hide when I'm visibly upset like I could before. The worst part is I'm back to being alone, doing it again all by myself, and that is where things went sour the first time.

I cannot get over the negative thoughts about how much I've lost while in the program, but I need to reflect on what it has helped me achieve, or at least experience. Most of the change occurred during, and immediately after, my intervention. By reviewing my 8- week stay there, I think I need to view pros and cons of the program in hopes that I can work on the cons and take pride in the pros.

PROS:

1.   I have felt things that I have not felt in years due to suppressing them. Even feeling the bad ones and reacting to those in a way that everyone else reacts must be beneficial for me with feeling human.

2.   I was given the chance to try out the intervention. I lasted much longer than I thought I could, so maybe next time I can last longer. It was pure fucking hell to say the least, but I was in a supportive environment where I could express what the intervention was doing to me.

3.   Picked up an old passion again I never thought I would-badminton. I gave it up when I was ten years old because my dad has his brain injury and I used to play it daily; I had forgotten how much fun it was until I played again.

4.   The other patients here are truly phenomenal and the most well-rounded and caring people I have ever met. Some of them I hope to keep in contact with for a long while. Even if I lose contact with any of them, they will never be forgotten. They've been the first people ever to show me the real meaning of *inspiration*.

5.   I don't question my feelings… well, not nearly as much. I'm more accepting of them and when I can't quite figure out why I'm feeling a certain way I don't dismiss it. I look at the evidence and come up with a rational and valid conclusion every time. Every feeling I have is justified instead of dismissed, even if it makes no sense at all.

6.   Through the intervention, I saw a clear face for the first time since I was a small child. Not only was it physically uplifting, but it signified that yes **I can** do it.

7.   I made a connection from my mind to my body during the intervention. I thought it was BS at first, like how exactly would I know when I "connected"? But I wasn't dissociated during the intervention and had to make that connection… the awareness to my body that no, I wasn't going to touch it. I wasn't going to touch *me*.

8.   I'm still alive despite my crash this past Saturday and am going through my worst depression ever. If I crashed and had NOT been in the program I probably would have attempted to take my life again.

9.   Lately I've been more accepting of certain personality traits I despised because I know these will never change and are actually the foundation to something better… though I'm still searching for that something.

10.   I'm not as revolting internally and externally like I thought, along with others from my past. It's too tiring to think like that all the time and as low as my self-esteem is now, it is better than before I started the program because it was downright scary, now that I look back.

CONS:

1.   I can't hide my pain anymore- maybe I can pick that ability up again but have to learn to use it when appropriate instead of all the time.

2.   I'm more self-conscious of my body through new revelations (not bad necessarily, but…new) and of my feelings. It connects to how much differently I will be viewed when classmates see and talk to me again, which frightens me.

3.   "Friends" dropped like flies on dog shit for too long. The upside to it is that they are potentially toxic and not what I really need and the few friends who have stuck by me are valued even more. I'm acknowledging the loneliness now more than ever, but maybe it's for the best because I can do something about it.

4.   Now that I'm experiencing emotions, they are random and I could be ok one second then near tears in the next. I really don't like not having control, as people already know.

5.   I don't have false self-confidence anymore, which is how I've been acting in theatre. I don't have real or false confidence but if I learn one of the two skills, I definitely want it to be the first. Right now I cannot imagine doing about 75% of the things that I did in Improvisation in the past.

6.   My depression has hit probably the hardest yet and I am bringing people down around me, though I'm told it's ok to do that? Not a concept I'm 100% for. I just can't hide it all the time anymore.

7.   What can I do with my immediate future… what choices do I really have?

8.   Black and white thinking hasn't changed and I really wanted it to. It's always all or nothing.

I'm making this entry because my main purpose of going into the program was to receive help with my disorder. I now understand that I could never have gone through an intervention without the professionals trying to crash the metaphorical wall to my emotions first. It was a process to get me to the point where I had to try, to gain enough confidence to say that I could do it. I always have dismissed my dreams in life because dreams are wants and wants are signs of vulnerabilities. In relation to my picking and what I want for myself, I should claim what I want. Even the things I'm embarrassed about, because they are justified and these wants won't go away if I ignore them:

- To one day give myself a beach day, whether it's alone or with a friend or two. Lie down on a sandy towel, wearing a bikini, and bask in the sun without caring about my scars.

- To be able to walk into my bathroom without having the need to pick. To look into the mirror and not immediately think something negative.

- To not hate the damage already done to my skin enough to start forming quality relationships- better friendships and maybe even a relationship.

- To eventually learn that intimacy is a way of expressing intense and positive feelings, not be scared that it's a tool of manipulation used to cause pain. I want to be comfortable enough in my own skin to be in a physically vulnerable scenario as a willing participant.

- To take pride in any accomplishment I make so that I can gain more confidence to achieve my ultimate goal of not picking.

- To start making people around me genuinely happy, but to ensure that this time it's me SHARING happiness instead of emitting false happiness to please others.

- (In later years) To accept the fact that this degenerating chapter in my life existed and take pride in overcoming my largest hurdle ever.

- I want my heart to start making some decisions for me instead of my head because I'm missing out on a lot. I also want to show love to the people I appreciate without fear, and be able to stay true to myself by doing the same for me.

Forever I want to believe that things will be ok in the end. Forever I want to live in this moment thinking that things just might work out. That not everyone is shallow, that my accomplishments aren't taken in vain. That my heart can be trusted and when it can't, that my mind will get me out of trouble instead of avoiding all possibilities to begin with. I want to be able to put a smile on people's faces again, but also put a smile on my own; not just be remembered as the girl who could make you smile when she's crying on the inside. I want out of this torment- and in this moment I believe it will happen; that I can finally bring myself to life. Be the girl everyone wants to be around because she is genuinely content with herself and her surroundings. I want to taste true love, just once, even in a passing moment, to know that it exists and can be attained... for me. And smile when I see myself in a picture, a picture where I'm not trying to hide an imperfection or hide behind other people.

If believing all of this puts me in an uncomfortable and vulnerable position, then maybe I do want to be vulnerable forever; if pure emotional exposure opens me up to happiness, then I am willing to let my guard down. This is the forever I want and as unrealistic as all of these goals combined are, maybe I can take one goal at a time so that I will always have something to strive for.

Nothing Lasts Forever   *08-26-2006*

I'm trying a semi- intervention again, meaning I'm going to try to stop picking my face, shoulders, and upper chest. My legs will be my "retreat", if you will. For the last few days I can't grasp why I keep slipping up so often- it's as if I never even promised myself to stop. Looking back on my 9 day ordeal I can't fathom how I'd only pick about

3 or 4 spots in one day... that's fucking amazing! Well, it w**as** amazing. I don't know what my drive was then or how I was able to motivate myself to go through with the insanity part of it. It just doesn't seem possible, yet I think I owe it to myself to try again because I was able to do it once. It feels like I ruined *my only chance* to get better because I couldn't control my moods, so I gave up… to then be booted out of the program after. I know that if I were to have continued the intervention they would have kept me an extra week just for the moral support I needed. It's a fact that I'll never have that many professionals on a "team" for me or that much support from a group of individuals. I'm back to being me- alone, fighting this struggle silently and I don't even like talking about it anymore because I feel like I've milked it for what it's worth. There's no sense in whining about something that isn't changing, something that won't go away easily, if at all. It was bittersweet and new to me to talk about Dermatillomania to people other than my immediate family, so it was a bit of an ease to be able to speak candidly and not be viewed as a freak.

In a week and a half I'm going back to university- I am not qualified to receive a disability pension because of a fucking disorder that isn't known by many professionals. The pension would be viewed by shallow individuals who'd say, "*Hmmm... picking skin... this girl can stop and she'll be fine*". Well, geez, I have heard that plenty and even from a "professional". To know I'm going to be rejected for disability hurts me so much because I actually thought this would be my year to finally tackle this disorder and get it under control. I would like to control it before it takes over my life and before it affects every facet of my existence… but wait, it already has. My sister is on disability for a universally well-known

95

issue and the government tells her that she's worth the time to get better... but I'm not? I'm so jealous and sometimes even get angry about it because she doesn't know how lucky she is. Now I'm being thrown into school before I can gather the pieces the program broke me into when now, more than ever, I want to get better. I must dispose of those thoughts because in order to function in life without being a neurotic mess, I have to pick at my skin to survive.

I have no choices. I need to pay rent and by going to school I am able to receive that money from my father's disability. To not go to school because I'm so caught up in my own superficial insecurities? With being so upset about my infinite amount of scars, I need to weigh what's more important- taking time off to make myself stop something that no one else does or go back to school and get an education so that I can do something with my life? Honestly, at this point, education means nothing to me. I was given a glimpse of another chance at life while in the program, and I want it. I don't know what "it" is exactly, but I know it has nothing to do with school and little to do with socializing... but it's what I'm striving for. How can I get something that I don't even know what it is? How is that even possible?

This illness runs in my family. My sister and I both have it, but hers is not nearly as severe as mine- hers is only on her face and occasionally on her back plus she knows when to stop. Like me, it's gratifying for her to pick her skin. The other day she told me she wanted to stop to know what it was like for me. She knew it wouldn't be as hard as it is for me since mine is completely out of control, but I don't think she lasted more than three days... and she couldn't do it. Now she doesn't nag at me as much when I'm occupying the washroom, unless I'm in her way while she's getting ready for bed... but she understands how hard it must be for me, to a degree. I'm grateful that she wanted to find a way to relate to me.

I was told that I'm getting a cognitive behavioral therapist. At first I was told that there are none available in my area but then I found out that there are a few residents are in the hospital and need to take on patients one at a time. So, the psychiatrist at the hospital (where I went to the program) said I'm the perfect candidate. It doesn't hurt to try it out. The other day I decided that I needed a change to try and perk myself up, give myself a reason to stop picking- purely for the superficial "I want to look like a human" need. I want to see myself like how I was starting to look when the redness and lesions were going away and I was able to stroke a smooth face. So I bought hair dye, colored my hair bright red and bought a bit of makeup. In order to start feeling good about yourself, you need to focus on the emotional/ mental/ psychological aspects of the change- sometimes just a shift in appearance can be a slight motivator.

Picking is a full-time job. It's constantly on my mind. I'm always trying to tell myself not to do it, stop it, don't go into the bathroom, keep myself occupied, and I just don't know how I'm going to manage that stressor plus schoolwork. Although it is my worst enemy, picking is also my best friend and in a way I don't want to lose that friend who has been there through all of my darkest times, who has helped me write my essays, who I confide in when I'm upset and don't want to bother anyone else with my issues. It's similar to eating disorders, regarding the power struggle- we feel in control of our actions but in reality we are overpowered by the disorder because it's an addiction that needs serious help in reversing.

Time, Why Do You Punish Me?   08-27-2006

It seems like time passes much faster when I'm isolated in the washroom picking my skin. Minutes go by, an hour or two go by, sometimes even longer, and it only seems like a moment has passed instead. Just like a video game that you get hooked to as it reels in your concentration and dedication, you can play it for hours and soon it's bedtime. By doing what I have for years and accumulating the hours I have spent on myself in this respect, I have wasted quite a large chunk of my life- possibly seven months straight without sleeping, if I made an estimate. When time passes quickly and it happens all the time, I miss out on many opportunities, possibilities, and I fall further away from my dreams. Sometimes I feel younger than I am because I have missed out on a lot of my life by not taking chances or doing anything positively risky due to my own self-hatred and lack of confidence/ self-worth, so I have not made mistakes to learn from. I haven't given myself the opportunity to mature because I have not shown courage to take chances. I'm scared to death because the odds are against me when it comes to succeeding… but I guess overcoming fear is the definition of being courageous.

The life I'm living this present day is not the absolute best, but it's been the best that I can remember. I'm not being pressured to socialize but yet I do have the opportunities to socialize and know how to set my

98

limits if I don't want to hang out with people. I'm taking it easy though I'm challenging myself daily to lessen the severity of my disorder. That will abruptly stop come **Sept. 6th** when I must focus on my schoolwork and a few of my close friends are moving away. I hate how my gut is telling me that going back to university is like throwing myself in a pit of hungry wolves. It's a kamikaze mission like every other year since I'm forced to hide all of my problems and go to classes, face my social anxieties, etc. Every year the same struggles get worse and it's harder to do these mundane tasks. By being in the program for 2 months and being shown that things can get better if I work on them, and then not get the choice to... I know I'll crash because I let this only chance of getting better slip through my fingers. It's one or the other- school, work, or disability, but I can't get disability and I need money for rent... so I must live life the way I have for years.

Look where it has gotten me. I am terrified about my future. I want time to stop just so I can live in this limbo because I know with time progression comes responsibilities I may not be able to live up to.

- CHAPTER III: A Deepening Depression -

There's No Escaping   *08-31-2006*

*N*ighttime. It's all about the darkness of the night that brings about most of the darkness of my thoughts. It's been more so lately and I've been dreading being awake past 10pm when the sun is completely down and life itself goes into a momentary hibernation. Yet when these thoughts arise, I know that the daytime is what hides my inner thoughts which are bombarded by hopelessness and fears. By focusing on the sun, communicating with others, and even hearing the neighborhood kids playing outside, I'm not left alone with myself.

I don't know if I try to reduce my situation to absolute absurdity or if I'm really giving myself a reality check but the worst occurs when I'm lying in my bed trying to sleep. The past few nights I've played my favorite band to go to sleep but I instead focus on the lyrics and find the correlation between their messages and my life. Most of the turmoil in my situation which I'm conflicted about is the way I view it. While in the program I gave myself hope that I could be accepted by other people for this disorder, that I wouldn't be viewed too abnormally- just simply as a normal person with a peculiar problem. Every night, the more I fight with myself in the bathroom and end up losing to the temptation of relieving my stress, the more I see myself as a failure. Ugly. Again, I've been trying to disconnect my mind from my body to see what other people would see if they saw *me*, in full, for the first time. Normally if I'm able to not pick as much, even in one area, I see progress but when I view it from what I see as another person's perspective, I'm still a freak.

I was told before by someone in the program that I'm way too hard on myself about the past scars I have, but I'm really not. They are partially what prevent me from being emotionally open with people because I cannot be physically close to them and have it own any meaning. Not in the sexual sense but I love giving and getting hugs, but they have been so empty for so long. It's the physical touch that gives me validation that at least the person who hugs me doesn't think I'm too revolting to avoid touching. I've been trying to develop emotional relationships with people, to strengthen what I have with everyone and what hurts is they are distant from me... so I want to stay the same. The reason why no one listens to my problems is because they've been the same ones for years and they can't be fixed- at least their problems are simply questions and answers which can be resolved in a timely manner. My main problem is an open wound.

Overall, I've been feeling much more ugly than usual. I see my wounds as other people would see them- very... disgusting, unnecessary. Like my view of myself. These nighttime hassles have been becoming progressively worse and lead my mind to the ultimate "only" ways of fixing the problem. Why can't therapists just put me in a fucking induced coma for a few weeks and then work on cognitive behavior therapy afterward? My legs are a lost cause in terms of scarring but I want to save the rest of my body. I can't keep living like this, being so ugly- that's not even the real term because it doesn't describe how subhuman I feel with my appearance. I admit a large insecurity with that is that I can never date because I couldn't show a partner my unclothed body and expect him to be turned on. Just by showing a guy my legs before being in an intimate situation will fuck up any chance of intimacy. That's why I try to suppress those feelings. I want to look at my scars how society views a burn victim's scars- just different, not necessarily gross. But with me, I'm continuously burning myself and life keeps throwing on the gasoline.

Dating is not a priority at all, but it leads up to my future and the fact of how long I've been single. I'm going to be alone forever. I'm very insecure and anti-social lately, plus school is in a week. I'm fucked. This is the attitude I'm going to have to hide, and pretend that I don't even have a disorder that eats me up everyday, though it's what controls me and unfortunately defines me as a person. My life is going to become a crock again just so that I survive my third year of university.

Deliverance   *09-01-2006*

I need to make an apology to anyone who has read this journal and heard about my trials and tribulations with this disorder, along with the momentary accomplishments I made which had me end up in a worse state than I started off in. I'm sorry that I'm not any sort of inspiration in overcoming this illness; it doesn't help others gain hope in battling their own issues. I'm sorry that I won't be the first person to

The happy family before Dad's brain injury (picture taken in 1995)
L-R: Dad, my sister, Mom, me

Our new life (picture taken in 1999)
L-R (clockwise): Me, Mom, my sister, Dad

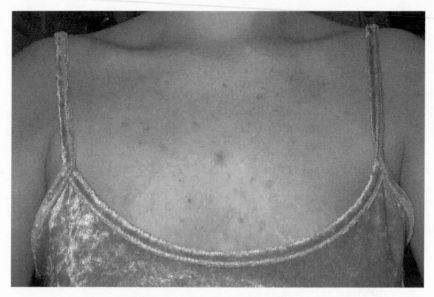

My upper chest (Dec. 15th, 2006)

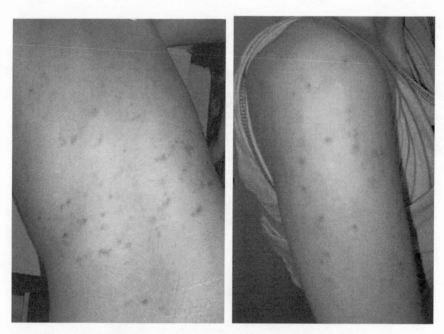

My back before the tattoos (April 26th, 2006) and my arm (Jan. 18th, 2007)

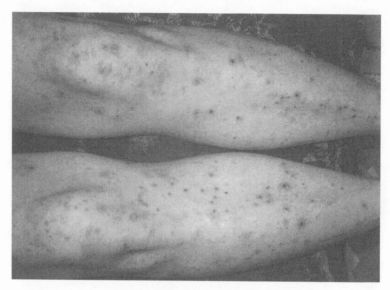

My legs (April 15th, 2007)

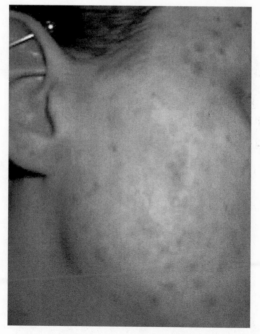

One side of my face (also April 15th, 2007)

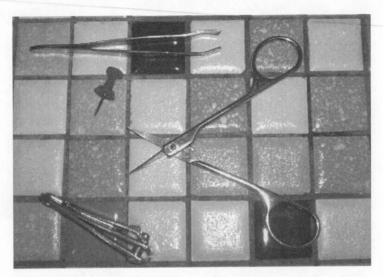

The tools I use to pick at my skin

Where I spend most of time picking. My back left an imprint on the wall from leaning on it

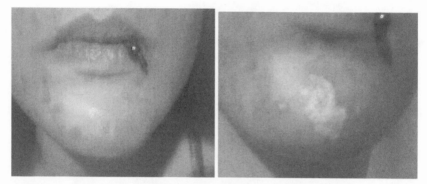

The infection I woke up with (left), and then I picked at it and put peroxide to try and clean it (right)

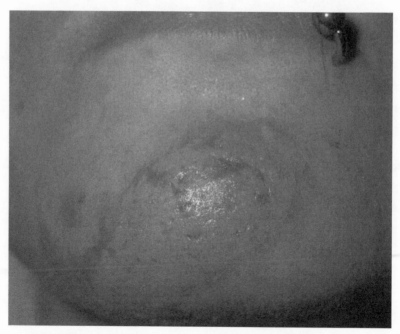

When I used a tack to poke at my chin in a failed attempt to drain it

Professionally taken by Wayne Forrest (Feb., 2008). A way for me to begin accepting myself.

overcome this illness although I so badly wanted to be- I just know I can't do it.

I don't have motivation anymore, for this or anything else. After that full intervention I had hope that I could do it again in due time because I had managed to mostly stop picking for nine days straight. The fall was much worse than one I experienced before... it was different. Since then I've been trying to find reasons to get better and jump back on the bandwagon, but I'm exhausted and really don't see a meaning to anything anymore. It isn't even depression, it's just reality. It is too bad that people frown on me for being so negative and cynical because they believe that there is a fix, even if it's extremely difficult, there's a fix for everything. Even if it is true, I've put in everything I have and it obviously means nothing and it was never good enough.

Every emotion I suppressed has come out and each one makes my brain ache. Even happiness because it's only a passing moment plus it has its downfalls, meaning someone has to be uncomfortable or hurt in order for me to be happy because my emotions are inappropriate. I now feel these emotions but cannot express them or even talk about them- I've shut down. I'm tired of burdening my friends, though the program told me it's a gift to share my troubles with people. Sharing and bombarding are two different things and I'm doing the latter. I bring everyone around me down and it hurts me that I am, in fact, this kind of person because I've always wanted to inspire and give hope.

I don't want to fight anymore. In reality, I do want to die. I can't fight this pain anymore and I wish now more than ever that my suicide attempt had worked because I've been fed false hope since then that brought me up a bit to only fall back into what is true. I'm sadistic, depressing, and unable to love or get close to anyone and really, who would want to get close to me? I push people away, it pisses them off, they admit they don't understand but wish they could help me, and they stay away. This is the way it's always been and I just can't change this. The rare times real emotions have been brought out of me, I distanced myself from the sources because it scared me. The program brought emotions out of me and now I'm so vulnerable, so damn needy which I'm not used to being at all. That neediness in itself pushes people away so I'm just going to get back into my usual lingo.

I had a dream once that I was in a washroom stall by myself. My hair was stringy, greasy, and hanging loose. I was in a cramped stall near a window and had a shotgun. I put the gun in my mouth and pulled the trigger, heard the bang, but wasn't in pain and was perfectly ok. It angered me so I did it again, same thing, and again, and I heard people screaming, telling me to stop. Blood was spreading on the walls of the stall but I just didn't die. I was crying by the second bang, just because I was so frustrated that I was still alive and nothing I could do would end it.

Tonight I was going to do what I usually do when I feel this hopeless and have nothing to turn to- write letters to people and call myself out, possibly sometimes calling them out on their actions. I'll say everything I fucking have to say then tell them all to stay away from me because I'm only capable of harming them and myself. I do have a lot of compassion in me but it doesn't know how to come out and it's too overwhelming. By hiding my emotions in the past, I never actually felt them. Feeling them would only bring me to my suicidal snaps and I swear I'm trying hard to fucking hold on right now. I now cry more over

110

this chronic emotional pain which hurts so much. I hate crying and cannot cry in front of people and I figured out why; when I cry I need to be held like a child- not even talked to, not be given false encouragement... just being accepted for the mope I am. Sometimes a gesture is more than what words could ever say.

Maybe I'll walk down to the hospital and tell them to put me in a fucking coma before I attempt it myself. Put me out of my misery for a while and maybe when I wake up I can feel like a human. A human who is entitled to emotions, a human capable of being cared for instead of distanced from. That or they can shock my brain a few thousand times until I forget the function of picking, or forget what it's like to hurt like this. I won't try to kill myself again but how nice it would be to get hit by a bus or have some other tragic accident happen. The only thing keeping me in this misery right now is that I have a few family members who love me and would miss me if I were dead. It makes me feel like being here is so selfless on my part and if they really loved me and accepted reality that things won't get better, they'd let me go. They'd let me move on to something better because surely things cannot be worse than this. The emptiness and frustration of not being able to communicate clearly and effectively with others, or even relate to them is too much. I'm not able to pick up the phone right now and tell someone I need an ear to listen to me. But I also wouldn't want to hear that things will be alright because I've heard that lie more times than I can count.

I can't shake off the feeling of being a freak. I don't think I've ever felt this revolting in my life and I don't want to leave my house because of it. One wish I have is to not hate sexual feelings or thoughts because of the frustration that I will never have that chunk of my life fulfilled. Not even one night. I wanted the program to help me accept this part of me but they wanted to do the opposite and raise my self-esteem to feel confident enough to "put myself out there", but I never did. They didn't want to help me accept that so now I'm even angrier that there's a sliver of me beneath the internal ugliness screaming to experience passion just once more so I CAN move on. All of these emotions are out and I want this emotion taken care of; I swear I wouldn't be greedy- just once so that I know what it's like to be wanted by a partner. Not even for sexual gratification, but to just hold someone in full form.

There's nothing in this life that can come near to mimicking the closeness of 2 heartbeats mirroring each other and 2 pairs of eyes reading much deeper into each other, reading each other's minds. Feeling breath brushing softly against your skin followed by reassuring tender kisses and arms wrapped securely around your waist. Not just being touched but knowing where your hands belong in the moment, knowing the right speed and genre of the touch. To have hands confidently roam every crevice of your body followed by soft lips copycatting the actions while savoring the moment; touching sexually, romantically, even friendly. This fantasy is too far- fetched to occur, so I want to forget these needs again because I was so damn close upon entering the program. It hurts because I'm too physically unappealing and I know attitude is a large influence in picking a mate, but I lack there as well. I want to write my close friends, even apologize for not being the best friend to them that every person needs but even more I wish I could express this in person. It's not that I clam up or get scared, but the words don't flow or even enter my mind to share. Basically, I'm more aware of my faults that have resulted in my

112

screwed-up relations with people or lack thereof. It's a burden to me to ask for a hug instead of receiving one out of the blue (which I used to get all the time from people) and this summer everyone has remained so distant since finding out about me going into the program. There's something about skin on skin contact that is electrifying; it validates that I'm alive and can feel warmth somehow. While picking my skin I don't feel alive, I feel so disconnected, but if someone else even touches my shoulder I feel like I'm grounded on this earth. Like I'm really here and have as many rights as someone else. Sick thinking but it's mine nonetheless. I know that this disorder has changed my way of thinking, making it spiral downward and when it comes to sexuality, I think I have what is called "Affectional Orientation" where I cannot initially be physically attracted to a male, only drawn in by emotions and some sort of mental relation. My own physical insecurities have me unable to be sexually attracted to a "hot" guy... and it's alienating since I see all my friends pursuing people when I stay away.

I've been trying in the friendship department but I'm still the same to my friends. I'm the lost cause friend who is not well understood, but universally known as a doomed fuck-up; someone who friends can turn to for advice but not be able to return because of their own emotional capabilities, but they are the lucky ones. Now I'm more aware of my picking, especially since the intervention when I lived minute by minute watching my every move and hoping not to fuck up. Now I know when I do it but just don't care enough to stop. I'm on a high dosage of my pill, but this is the millionth drug I've been on. It's too bad my current professionals aren't telling me that they have no fucking clue what they're doing because they want me to think they have ideas up their sleeves. They're just throwing shit at me to keep me alive because I am at my wits end. I told myself upon entering the program that this would be my last resort and if nothing changed, I'd be gone. But I'm here, only holding onto this shell of mine because other people want it around.

Now I think the best thing I can do is push everyone away. For their good; to do what's best for the people who have treated me the best because they don't deserve to have me bringing them down. I don't even want to go online or anything. I want people to forget me or when I'm only a distant memory, they can look back and see at me as the failure, the one they all wonder if she changed her life around... but probably know nothing will save her. Writing goodbye letters to my friends would make them think I'm killing myself and they wouldn't understand until their lives progress without me, that it's best that I'm out of it. This approach is to fade away and, God, there are a few people I don't want to let go because they've been inspirational and influential but those are the same reasons I need to let them go right now. Maybe one day my mood can be maintained and I can accept my scars/ disorder but I have not even seen that day let alone the day when the disorder is gone.

Everyone wins this way. Either way I'm going to lose, but I don't want the people I care about to also lose. My family won't go away so they've purchased a losing ticket but maybe one day they'll see that I'm suffering and let me go. At this point I can only wish that they'll let me go and realize that it can't get better for me. Until then, I am stuck here just existing and hating.

I hate being this person and having these sick thoughts that I know aren't right to have, but yet I know there is truth in it. The truth

114

hurts but now I am more aware of what I'm capable of and I've been shown true moments of happiness where I've forgotten about everything ugly and been close to convinced that there is a solution to this problem through hard work. I always fall back to this because this is who I am. I'm being forced to go back to school just to get money for rent, but maybe I won't go because fuck knows I can't right now. Would my mom kick me out? No- but I would have to starve or something. Fine with me, it's just another way of me withering away. I'd have no health insurance anymore so I would also stop taking my meds due to the cost.

I can't live this anymore. I'm so alienated, alone, isolated, filled with self-hate, and I can't express anything good to people because my cynicism always gets the better of me. With being more acquainted with the negatives in life, it's easier to communicate that than the positives. I really wish I didn't enter the lives of the amazing people I have because I haven't been able to reciprocate hope with my own actions and behaviors. I'm sorry to everyone, but right now I know only a few of you can read this. There's no sense in updating this anymore- maybe some day but everything seems pointless right now. I really wish things were different, that my brain was reconfigured because I know deep down I could be a powerful and influential person if I wasn't so down and fucked up. What to do from here is a mystery because things cannot change but I must stick around.

Who knows- maybe I'll come back to this journal, maybe even in a few more days just so I can hold onto something. I hope that one day a professional will look at this journal and take this disorder seriously enough to look for a cure or a way to maintain it. That won't happen in my lifetime so I just don't know what to do because I am not able to live; I'm only able to exist miserably.

In and Out of Doubt   09–06–2006

When I am content with an accomplishment that I recognize, I try to bathe in the achievement for my own self. When I am depressed I start by narrowing down a few reasons why I am depressed, and then I end up remembering and blaming myself for all my past failures.

Everything I wrote in my last entry is still true, even if I have came out of my dark depression. I still think that I am better off dead and wish that my loved ones will see that instead of keeping me around for their selfish needs (for a lump of company). I am still in a state of dysphoria that has been with me for over half of my life, so being content (for me) is being able to manage my emotions and not let them get the best of me. I still view my existence as being bleak and meaningless because I have screwed up all chances of happiness with this disorder. There's no chance to be myself, no chance to make emotional connections, romantic/ sexual connections, for a stable mental health outlook with a positive self-image. How can a person look at a body like mine with all its wounds and then tell me that I should love this shell? It would be hypocritical for someone to say that because if someone had my body plus the shame of not being able to stop this harmful action causing the wounds, that person would develop a deep self-hatred as well.

The main focus of the day treatment program was for patients to feel their emotions and own them. When I first entered, I didn't realize how emotionless I was and how robotic my actions were. Into my third week I started cracking because of the frustration behind how alienated I felt from myself, so I yearned to know what it was like to feel. Seeing people read letters in group with tears streaming down their faces moved me immensely- it is the most powerful human emotion. So pure, vulnerable, and HONEST. Sharing truths proves how courageous and unafraid to face demons the patients there were and I have so much admiration for those qualities. Not that I'd prefer to see people cry over laugh, but we see too many masks and plastic smiles so it's hard to tell what's genuine. It's more difficult to lie in a tear than to lie on a smile. On the other hand, I would read my letter[s] but not feel because I haven't for so long that I really forgot how to. I shook while reading my introduction letter and my voice quivered but there was... nothing. I had to even ask myself if I was feeling but just didn't know it.

Since the intervention I've been a train wreck of emotions; taking everything personally, being needy of advice and reassurance, and I despise those needs because they interfere with other people. Every emotion was harmful to me because when I felt happiness, I would be greedy and want more. Each facet of my life is painful and I really cannot deal with that pain. Even before my most recent deep depression I felt myself distancing emotionally from people I was starting to connect with at SOME level. For the last few days I've felt nothing again, just like a zombie. With that ability though, I am able to suck it up and go to school which I have to do no matter what, plus I don't have to bug people for the sake of dependency.

Without any feeling of happiness I don't have to face the downfall of my hopes and my crashes will come less frequently. On the downside, without having aspirations occupying my mind, my motivation is lacking and I really am empty again. I don't think these decisions are made consciously- I believe my sub conscious knows what's best for me in order to be able to live my life daily. I am unable to sit with pain because I'm too self-destructive and can't let go of it, plus the pain of not having my innermost dreams and desires fulfilled (because they never can be) is far more than I can handle. I just want to forget they exist and they haven't existed until I was given more false hope from the program. People have noticed that I've been more upbeat these last few days but that's because I now have a choice- to act miserable or act happy. It's better than being in an involuntary state of "being": To BE miserable or BE happy. This mind frame is much more accommodating for everyone since I won't need people to be there for me, and I don't have to sit with the shame of asking for help. The only thing I've held onto tightly is my independence, strong sense of power in decision making without being sidetracked by social inadequacies. But I want to feel happiness, just the warmth in my cheeks I had when I smiled in the last few weeks… but the repercussions aren't worth it. Without having a pure smile, I know I lost a gift that I can share to possibly create a connection through that simple gesture.

The last few days have been strange because I'm thinking it's wrong to go back into this detached state since my "retreat" was hammering in my head that my problem was dealing with suppressed emotions. My problems have been far worse since being able to feel emotion and not being able to control it. Life is heading for disaster and I can predict that my next fall will be at the end of the month when the realization that I am in fact trapped at school again sits in, along with a few other factors. For over a month, my mind has been boggled by an unknown concept- that there is in fact, something better out there and it feels like going back to school is drifting me further from that fulfilling life. I don't know if I've created a nirvana in my mind so that I'll always have a drive to search for it, but when I'm very depressed I start to believe that maybe I'm only dreaming about death. I can't fathom why I feel like school is holding me back from an unknown satisfaction.

Lately I've been able to make other people happier. I haven't been mad at someone I should be and have been laughing off his immature behavior and he's backed off. I'm so apathetic toward ill manners instead of taking it personally, unless it's me becoming more desensitized to social interactions and my overall distress. At this point, it doesn't matter if I feel emotions because I have this disorder no matter what. This is a loss to me so it's saddening that I can't let myself yearn solely because it hurts to dream. Just to be able to yearn without knowing that I'm the reason why I can't make something possible would be alright. To not be screwed up to the point where I can achieve the goals I long for is ideal, but it's be a foreign concept to believe that I can do some things other people can. My disorder has consumed me so it would be appalling for me to tell anyone about it because subconsciously I become a lost cause to someone: a sick child, a toxic influence, and an excuse for pity. I'm not seen as being strong, independent, or funny anymore. If I told people about my Dermatillomania, my name would only become associated to my disorder; by telling someone about it and how much it is my life now… it would be too hard for them to hear the name "Angie" without automatically thinking "Picking" or "Scarred".

Racing Through Quicksand   09-06-2006

It finally hit me that school is in less than 24 hours. The blow came hard and I had a severe crying spell in the bathroom for a good 10 minutes, followed by a few minutes of picking to regain my composure and put a face on for my family. I've told people that I'm choosing not to go back to school, just for tomorrow anyway, and my dear uninformed peers have been telling me that I'm "copping out" of returning, that I "have to do whatever, though it sucks", "am going back without a choice", etc. It's too fucking bad that these people don't know what I suffer from (*or do but don't clue into how hard it makes life*) nor do not they care that I was in rehab, but you know, everything is A-OK NOW! I am completely alone again with no one to talk to, no one with enough patience for the same old bullshit I spew all the time. No one even cares to know why I don't even want to go back- I'm automatically considered a slacker even though people know that something's wrong. But hey, every story MUST always have a happy ending so by me not conquering all of my demons in the program, my story is a mystery.

If I go tomorrow I'll crash, but I have to because my family is so fucking poor that I need to bring in the money for them. At this moment I don't want to hang out with or be near anyone because when I am, I end up feeling even lonelier in the end. The program isolated me because of my disorder, teased me with the fact that there's no cure but that they

120

could bring hope to a desperate little girl, and be close to people just to have it all torn away in a few weeks time. I'm back to being the same person I was before entering except my symptoms of everything is more accentuated and my drive to continue this life is cut off because I want something better than this, something that isn't even real.

I want a real friend who isn't burdened by my bullshit. I want someone I can make a call to when I'm feeling down, someone who will hang out with me during good times or bad, someone who I don't distance myself from because it hurts when I develop a connection. There's something so putrid in the way my brain is wired that prevents my social development to be normal. I'm going back to school expected to be a social uppity person like I was before. To cheer everyone around me up when they are having their problems, to make them smile, to listen to them... whether or not I'm doing a good job of hiding my own troubles. I can't hide anymore because it feels like everyone is able to peer into my soul and see all of my flaws.

It really feels like everything has been taken from me. The little bit of good the program did left me and the damage it did set in. I'm much more insecure, vulnerable, socially awkward, unable to communicate, moody, depressed, and hopeless, than before. It's as if people can detect my secrets when they look into my eyes for more than a comforting period of time and I feel powerless by backing down. Sometimes it feels like when I walk around, my whole body is exposed and they can see my scars- whether it's through my clothes, whether or not they can see me naked, or maybe they can just see them through the torment in my blackened eyes. I'm trapped in my emotions, all of my friendships are robotic, and my need to communicate is much higher but my ability to just shut down. These are things that cannot change and I have turned bitter from recognizing what I CAN'T do in the life, the bleak existence the program solidified for me. It hurts that people don't understand how much I feel like a failure to myself and if I don't go to school I'll be a failure to my family. I'm already a failure to myself but I can't let my family down. I'm way too negative for anyone to want to hang out with the "true" me, for anyone to want to sit down and listen to me bitch about my deformities both in disorder, genetics, and drug intake. I want to make people happy but can't when I pretend because my shell has caved in. I don't want to make other people miserable but it comes naturally to me because I'm not a person to look up to and admire. I don't even want to be admired, but just want people to be drawn and connected to me without me being a burden or any hurt involved.

Everything for me is black and white- and I'm in the dark. I don't know how much of any of this I can take. My own ability to keep moving on, the motivation, the pain, the loneliness... I don't know how to make anything better but everything I've tried has gotten me to this result, to what I am at this moment.

I'm terrified. Maybe by walking around campus solo or sitting in a seat with empty ones surrounding it, I'll burst into tears because I don't want to be alone. I don't want to destroy my life but this is the way it has to be. It hurts being a dreamer, deep, deep down. I am going to school tomorrow, even if I go home early. I hate that in my heart it's not what I want, nor is it good for me. But when nothing is good for me anymore, I have to do something drastic.

<u>PS</u>- I tried to open up to one of my best friends, just saying that I didn't want to go tomorrow because it feels like I fucked up my life and this won't make things better. He told me he didn't want to argue with me about it because I'll dismiss what he says and unlike me, he's trying to do something with his education. He doesn't want me bringing him down with negative thinking tonight, and then he fucking blocked me.

He's just the only one who has balls to say what everyone else wants to.

Surely There Must Be Something Better   *09-16-2006*

Why is it that I'm more afraid to live than I am to die? Is it because I know that by trying to live I will fail and I would gain more success in ending my life, something that right now is not truly mine anyway?

Backtracking to a few days ago, I went back to see my psychiatrist. She told me that there was nothing her clinic could do but refer me to a general cognitive therapist, which isn't even a cognitive **behavioral** therapist. This therapist is only available doing a group dedicated to treating anxiety with cognitive thinking... or something like that. It's basically a waste of my time but those classes are only offered the 2 days I go to school- so she said I can't go to it (obviously). I hinted at the fact that I can't go to school all day because I'm exhausted by the end of second class but she told me that I should spread out my classes 5 days of the week. First of all, it's not possible at this point with the requirements I need and secondly, I have extreme anxieties just when I wake up knowing that I have to go to school. So she concluded that I'll

123

have to deal with it and she is decreasing my meds down to nothing because I have had extreme side effects that I do not want at all:

1. Worsened depression
2. Increased anxiety
3. Even worse skin picking (has been extreme since the failed intervention)
4. Random twitches in body parts
5. Excessive sleeping

After that she plans on putting me on another drug but dared to try to persuade me that it isn't a good idea. Why? I will most likely gain weight on it. I just felt like taking a fit and telling her how much I don't fucking care about weight gain because at least with being overweight, I'd be normal. I wouldn't be so ugly if I was overweight without this disorder, which I'd rather prefer. Hell, let Jerry Springer knock down the walls of my apartment to get me out if that's what it takes, to gain that much weight. The new med will hopefully decrease all of the above mentioned symptoms. As for the skin picking... that won't go away. The psychiatrist told me to go back and see my case coordinator from the program because there's nothing else the clinic in my city can offer. Oh yeah, but again I shouldn't give up hope!!! Even if a new pill reduces the skin picking I am still left as a mutilator. Maybe I can go back to how I was immediately before the failed intervention. Riiight.

Yesterday I spoke to my case coordinator before playing ping pong with the guy I met there. She told me that the story behind getting me a student/ resident cognitive behavioral therapist is not possible because they need to learn with patients who have disorders that are easier to conquer. There is no one in the area to help me but she suggested the same guy mentioned above whom does the group work. This guy sees my sister for her ongoing issues and she's been with him in therapy for five years. He is only an average therapist without specialties for MY needs. I'm tired of having my hopes up like a vulnerable child when all these people are doing is passing me around and feeding me false information so that I don't give up and off myself. This is the only alternative, and I was told anyway that group work is not going to be effective for me because of the severity of my condition. The psychiatrist told me too the day I saw her that it probably wouldn't help to see him but it wouldn't hurt. She's wrong because the more and harder I try, the worse the plunge is when I am deemed a failure. I haven't internalized it yet... but I think it's sinking in that yes, this is it. This is all that life can be for me. I will be alone in friendships, alone without the chance of knowing what romantic love is, and alone while suffering in my head. How do I live like this, knowing that the rest of my existence will be empty and miserable?

Right after I talked to my case coordinator I flopped on the couch in the lounge and cried for about five minutes. I stopped in time to compose myself for when my friend came, then I acted happy, and we had a great ping pong day.

I've never officially gave up on life without attempting suicide. Even then I kept trying to work toward something better. Suicide is not about wanting to die, it's about trying so hard to live that when failure seems imminent, there only feels like one option left. Now there isn't anything better and since no one wants me to die for their selfish and non guilt-ridden reasons, I'm sticking around and emphasizing my burdening behaviors on them. I quit school today, which in itself is degrading to my character because I cannot do it; although I know it's not a question about my intelligence, it's the last thing I was able to hang onto. The only reason I forced myself to go to school for these last 14 days is because I can't afford to live without it. I get paid $200 by a government service to go to school because of Dad's brain injury. If I don't go to school, then I don't get that money. I don't care. I can't work, I can't go to school, and my mom refuses to ever kick me out so we're going to be in a tailspin of financial difficulty SO much more than usual... and I'll place all that blame on me. Hell, I'll just starve myself and waste away in my room.

Yesterday I called my old case coordinator while crying and begged her to ask the psychiatrist if I can be put in an induced coma. At this point because of its severity there is no known cure and treatments haven't worked. For the last few days I've been so much more revolted by my appearance than ever and don't leave the house unless necessary. If they put me in a coma for, say, 5 or 6 days and wake me up for two days I'll have less marks on me and I KNOW my mood will brighten and I'll have motivation. Looking the way I do now I have no motivation

126

because I just feel so damn disgusting and feel like a failure as a human being. Then I can be put in a coma again and look even better until everything is healed (*3 weeks maybe?*) and I can then start the fight with the disorder with being steps ahead. I'll find out by Monday but I can guarantee the answer will be no because it is considered to be unethical. If there are no other options, nothing else to try, nothing else that'll work, then where's the inconvenience? Professionals just keep waiting until the magical fairy- therapist comes along and pours sprinkles on my head with hopes of a hokey cure.

I don't know if the program ruined my life or if it just pointed out how I ruined my life and how it's not possible to do anything about it. I don't want to live anymore. I'm so distant from everyone; I've been ignoring the fact that I have no friends whatsoever- just acquaintances that I've purposely backed away from. My life is nothing right now- no school, work (*because I'm too fucked up right now*), no self-esteem, no will to live, no friends, and no realistic goals. I don't have the ability to maintain a connection with another human and it's supposedly a gift that I am able to with a rare kind of person. I'm too revolting, both body and soul, to ever be intimate with another person. Essentially, I've been an ugly disorder for far too long. A fucked up one.

It's Unkind to Everyone   *09-29-2006*

Erratic moods, back and forth. Yesterday was a perfect example but I hit an extreme low for about an hour and a half. That was when I came home from my theatre meeting and Mom hounded me about taking some pictures of me because she doesn't have any to give to family (*and she's stressed that I'm the only one in the family without pictures to distribute*).

So she took the pictures and I viewed them as she uploaded them to her computer. There was a lump in my throat from seeing the results and I felt almost embarrassed. I have to keep reminding myself that my mind is playing games on me, but usually photographs are kinder to me than my own reflection. Before I left the house today I thought I looked better than usual. Better, not spectacular, just to give me a little boost for the day. I didn't wear a dumpy tee shirt, but instead wore a nicer and flattering shirt with my black dress-up jacket over it. I ran into an old friend while out earlier and she didn't recognize me on the bus because she told me I looked like a model- I know I gave her a weird look but she said she was serious. Confidence booster there, even if I can't see what she did. Later on in the night I ended up looking at myself in the mirror after I got out of the shower and was able to completely detach from myself and my views. I was horrified when I realized that my upper arms are much more damaged than ever before, along with my upper chest. It wasn't too long ago that it "traveled" to those areas. I just feel so disgusting, unworthy, revolting. Not even ugly, but just infected with a disease eating at my skin when it really isn't the case unless my actions are a disease. My legs are wrecked to no return but I don't think I could continue living with myself if my upper arms and chest get to that point. I don't even know how this disorder "worsens" by making me focus on other body parts, but I do and it's beyond frustrating.

I went to see my case coordinator the other day and almost cried while in; the trigger was when she looked at me and said, "*I know that this is so hard for you, Angie*". The way she said it just choked me up for a moment. She's trying to hook me up with social assistance to be able to pay rent to my folks. As for my now non-existent medical plan, she informed me that I may be eligible for free samplers for pills. There are solutions to all of the superficial issues instead of a solution I want to the largest problem. My problem. All of these tiny issues wouldn't exist if there was an answer to explain my ultimate downfall. Today I was supposed to go in for routine blood work but decided against it. I've had this disorder for 7 years- it's not like they'll detect something in my blood now that's "AHA, THERE'S the problem". The coordinator also suggested that some specialist I've never heard of before may be able to see me, someone who can teach people how to put themselves in a coma-like trance. That's **not** what I meant when I told her I wanted in a coma, but I think she knows that already.

When I thought that skin picking ruled my life about 4 months ago, I was wrong. Now it is because I cannot even go to school, cannot work, be productive in society and give back to the world. I'm cooped up in a safety net... and it's still lonely, as it has been for many years now. It was only 2 years ago I was going to school full time and working full time. Then it was work full time in the summer, only school last September, work this summer, then 2 months of rehab, and now nothing. Maybe I'm slowly disappearing instead of getting worse. That concept would relieve me if there rang any logic in it. I need to hide from reality again but my eyes were opened this summer and now I'm scared to face everything. I'm terrified of the truths I have found out because they are things that cannot be fixed and I have to face the fact that I am too detached from everyone around me.

A Little Update   10-08-2006

My overall moods have been leveling out for over a week now.
They are more manageable, so this week treated me rather nicely. I think
it's because I'm keeping my medication dose steady instead of further
reducing it, like at the rapid pace my psychiatrist suggested. I've been
stressed out about finances and the assistance I will or will not get, along
with the bursts of debts coming to me now that I'm not in school. For
the most part it hasn't negatively thrown me off... but it has given me a
more "normal" stress, if there's even such thing anymore for me!

Not doing a whole lot around here since I've been out of school.
This week my upper chest and arms were healing but last night the
strong urge overcame me and I was picking for quite a long time.
Sometimes I can't narrow the need down to a particular mood because I
was ok, but thinking, but still generally ok. Three days ago I did a number
to my left eyebrow and it looks like a cheese grater got to it. It didn't
damage the muscle like it almost did last time but it's very scabby now
and I keep trying to remove the scab which causes a lot of bleeding since
I went pretty deep.

Each Day Feels Like it's Getting Worse   10-12-2006

I'm sitting in the stairwell of my building typing and trying to stop
the tears that are welling up in my eyes. It's not my stairwell to cry in nor
is this isn't my life to cry about anymore. I'm sick of the daily struggle to

survive... to survive peacefully and to just *be*. There's a spontaneous struggle thrown at me each day, specific ones different weeks, and then there are the problems that plague me daily.

Everyone is ignoring me. I don't want to sound like a whining child but I feel so damn alone over and over, even when life is "good". No one has been online for a long while. I knew this was coming though- everyone has mid terms which of course I don't because I **can't**. Tony from the day treatment program seems to have gone MIA, one of my close friends has just been doing his own thing with school/ music, and the list just goes on. I've tried reaching out a few times to a number of people, people who I haven't been in close contact with lately, but there's nothing to grab onto because everyone's moved on from me. I'm a lump, a useless piece of human material taking up space in a stairwell. I know I did all of this to myself but it doesn't help that it hurts and people are driven away by my strange existence. I can't depend on social interaction or throwing myself into the medical world to solve my problems so I shouldn't burden anyone at all- it doesn't fix anything. Staying at home is sucking any bit of life out of me but where do I go if I leave the house? The only outside I've seen all week is from the front of my building, which is where I go out for my smokes. Yeah, that's nice thing to look forward to. Even if I am able to balance my moods again, I need to recognize how much of a problem I am to everyone else. How I piss people off by pushing them away or somehow piss them off and have them push me away.

The best thing to do tonight is go to sleep, like I do every time I fall into a dark depression and hope that the morning will help to maintain my usual dysphoria. It's tiring living like this when I can barely remember the times in my life that were considered ok. Why are two tears coming down from my left eye and none from the right? Isn't the idea of the perfect life smothered in structure, stability, but furthermore, equilibrium? Everything is so grim that it seems that something as simple as tears are fucked up too... tears that have now wet a line down the left side of my scratched- up face, unjustified tears, tears that I wouldn't shed before. Now the fight is keeping them in along with my sanity. This surely can't be from two nights ago when I reduced my meds by half instead of by a quarter. I waited long enough to reduce again and most doctors say to reduce by that much anyway. Could this also be why for 2 days straight I have not kept any of my food down, because I am bombarded with anxiety that makes me "thankful" (*in the most cynical way*) that I dropped out of school this semester? Yesterday I managed to sleep in until 5pm and hoped that my exhaustion would be enough to make sure I never wake up. My face is a mess but somehow my upper chest is damn near healed. My arms are very close to healed too somehow but the scars are far worse than I thought.

My new fixation is with body hair. Anything uneven or out of place has to go but with scissors instead of tweezers which is where I have run into most of my problems. It's probably why other parts of my body are healing, because it's a newer fixation. My legs are already unsalvageable but if I can be happier with 50% of my body (*not the 50% which the legs take up*) - it's better than giving up completely. This is all talk because I feel like I have given up on everything and have turned into a needy and blubbering baby. The only person we can all count on is ourselves for independence but when I cannot do that and want to reach out, nothing is inside of me except for weakness. I am blessed for the

132

amazing people in my life, but unfortunately when they view me I'm the opposite- a burden. Pessimistically looking at the brighter side of this, the few escaped tears of tonight probably tired me out enough to not have an all-out slaughter fest on myself.

To A Place in My Head   10-19-2006

So there was my dip from dropping my meds. I'm dropping one more time starting tomorrow night, then in another week's time I'm dropping to nothing for 2 weeks until my next appointment (doctor's orders). I'm going through such a hassle to get Social Assistance. It's embarrassing because I want to be like my friends- in school, maybe working, but instead I am feeling useless, begging for something that I wish I didn't have to get: Money for my incompetence. My psychiatrist wants to put me back on the pills I was on three years ago since it worked the best, but it the dosage was never maxed out. I was then switched in Dec. '04 which sent me into the most destructive/ embarrassing time of my life that I'd rather not remember existed. I'm still trying to recover from what I did to myself then- the drugs, different forms of self-harm, attempted rape, fling (*for the wrong reason*), loss of friendships, and suicide attempt.

My arms still look like hell from the damage I did starting around January of this year. I'm feeling more proud feeling better about my body because I've been trying to exercise daily for about two weeks now. Since my body is easy to shape up my stomach is already forming into a nicer silhouette which makes me feel overall better about myself and in control. I went to the second hand clothing store by myself and tried on some shirts that show my upper chest- no cleavage, just not shirts that touch my throat. It sunk my higher spirit because I don't look how I want to, but I never will because it's realistic. I have scars from when I was 8- 10 years old with acne on my upper chest and back, but then I look back and wonder how much of that was picking and how much was acne. I picked at the acne which could have started the original destructive trend.

Moods... well, have again been up and down. Never "up" enough to say I'm happy, but it's enough to go on without wishing for death to come ASAP. The ups come from my body image but the downs come from how much I've fucked up my life and how I can't maintain friendships/ go to work/ go to school/ have no career oriented goals anymore. Maybe, realistically, if the picking was to ever miraculously stop (hahaha), my problems would still be there. My psychiatrist keeps stressing to me, more than ever, that picking lets me avoid all of these problems... to actually *feel* them. While in the program I did feel, and it hurt, and it made me regress like I worried it would. I never thought I could get worse to not go to school but they did it to me and it's such a horrible feeling.

It's strange how my moods aren't matching up with my picking. It actually pisses me off because I can't predict when the "need" is, how often, or why. It's the why that bugs me because the need itself is truly illogical and I prefer to live life by facts. Another strange thought of mine is that I've never tried to lived life; I've always attempted to make it reasonable, logical, but I now know that doesn't lead to happiness. Every time I have tried to act with my heart, just for shits n' giggles, I've crashed hard.

My Favorite Disease   10-23-2006

I have concluded that the people who enter my life cannot be trusted. Every time someone enters I either throw them out but if they slip past my radar, they are the ones who end up hurting me. I tried many tactics of removing the "emotional pain wanted" sign off of my forehead but it just won't go away. I'm jealous of people who are able to form and maintain strong friendships- the ones based on trust, honesty, and openness because it's not me and when it is, I get hurt.

This leads me to believe that not all my problems are skin related like I want them to be. I want them to be because this disorder is such a defining influence in my life that without it, everything would be dandy. I can't decipher whether my personality provokes the disorder or vice versa because I want to blame my inability to connect with people and positively maintain anything on my disorder. That my scars make me so body- conscious and feel so unworthy as a human that I do not feel emotion like one, that I don't hold any human qualities- friendships, enemies, romance, spirituality. Really, I am a person and the program showed me how to hurt like a human instead of just knowing the pain is there and keeping it numb. It's hard to feel worthy of anything when I'm not respected so it would be better to be back and be an empty shell because emptiness is nothing except the hollow knowing that there is a better life out there that cannot be mine.

To talk about my traits of Body Dysmorphic Disorder, I am happier to report that overall symptoms seem to be getting better. I never made the connection to my sexual "attack" or whatever the hell you want to call it and those symptoms getting out of control until now. The program did help me deal with what happened because I never thought that it impacted my life so drastically. For a long time I have been convinced that I am way too ugly to date anyone, so ugly that no one would want to see my scars when it came time to intimacy. Just prior to the attack I had a fling with an older person and though I was self-conscious about the scars, I was able to still get into another person's bed so it had to have been after that that I was so convinced of my repulsiveness. While talking to someone a few weeks ago it was the first time I had thought about my fling but I later asked myself how I could have done that if I felt the way I do about myself now. I tried to reason with myself that it was a time of self-destruction... but I think things are different today in terms of why I've been avoiding any male relations. There's still a missing link when it comes to that because of my inability to connect with people and maintain a connection without emotionally withdrawing.

In these last three weeks I have been exercising daily and have been able to turn a great deal of my insecure belly pudge into muscle. Although my moods have been to extreme lows due to the reduction in medication, they have also picked up after the accomplishment of pushing my stomach muscles to the max. I do have some control and despite feeling completely fucked around by a great many of people, especially someone I was thrown off by, I do have control. Overall my picking has calmed down everywhere except my legs. I still cannot go a single day without picking every part I can get my frantic fingers on but I am not as torn to stopping myself as I was. I still don't feel pretty, but I feel deserving of love (*all forms*); though I always knew that... I never felt like it. It's a good feeling, but difficult to describe. Maybe someone reading this understands or hopefully will someday.

In conclusion, I'm finding inner strength. It's so painful not to have anyone to lean on for support but I must learn that even if I need people and they aren't there, I won't need anyone ever again if I keep on the way I am. Pure independence is a goal of mine; nevertheless, it does come with the negative price that I can't develop interpersonal skills. From my experiences, I'd rather suffer that pain than being walked all over. There aren't any more solutions- it truly is black and white. The program tried teaching me that sharing my problems with people is a gift to them instead of a burden, but it only sounds exquisite in theory. In practice, I am a nuisance and won't let myself open up again. I need to regain much more inner strength and overcome all social barriers like how I did before. I need to lay low and be the giver because I won't trust again.

But Where Do I Belong?   10-26-2006

I made video yesterday about my struggle with Dermatillomania and posted it online. I showed it (surprisingly) to my mom and sister. They were very shocked since I don't open up to them and they're still stunned by it. My mom started talking about how I should submit this to the news or something. I brushed her off immediately when she started mentioning it so I don't know exactly where she was going with it. Not every skin picker sufferer has had my life, but I think many can relate and I threw in some facts in the video as well.

I'm nervous about the reactions, but ready. I needed to make this for me. I don't know why, and I know the software program I used is a little cheesy, but I think the video is bold. Later on I'll probably make this video for private viewing only…

I met someone who was very dear to me. He's 26 years old, and I'm 20. We met in the program this summer and never in my life have I emotionally connected with anyone as intensely as I have with him. Yes there is sexual attraction toward him but I was just so in awe by him, and he's the first person who has ever actually inspired me to be the best person possible. I learned positive things about myself because I wanted to show him everything good about me since he had learned all of the screwed up things about me. I made extra efforts to make him smile because seeing that shy grin put me in such a great mood.

Three Saturdays ago the last thing he said to me via an IM service was "talk to you soon". I have not seen him online since, except for once last week when his status was set to "away" the whole time, which he never does. His cell phone is still connected when I called it last, more than a week ago. He's been putting off moving since he was supposed to be moving a few provinces away. Since the program ended, we've talked two or three times a week online and have seen each other at least once a week. The last 2 or 3 times we hung out he was extra-ordinarily happy to see me and hang out. He laughed more, smiled more, made more jokes and I didn't know where the change came from and neither did he. So why after getting even closer to Tony did this happen? Is this what happens every time someone gets close to me- I just get thrown aside? This is the first year of my life I've gotten closer to people, still with much disassociation. He moves me emotionally, I actually FEEL the emotion of caring, he inspires me with his constant attempts of getting better in comparison to anyone I've ever met in person, and I'm stimulated intellectually- basically in every way possible.

I'm so embarrassed and ashamed. He knew that two close friends of mine did this to me during the summer and he knows I don't let people get close to me. I had even told him that with the female (Jennifer), I would have liked to have been told that she didn't want to contact me, even without an excuse; just so I could know and not be left hanging six months later. I never expected this from Tony because his ex-girlfriend who he went out with off and on for eight years did this to him. My mom asked why I'm not going to the city to see "that boy" anymore and I told a white lie- I told her that he left. Well, he did, he left my life unexplained. He's not entitled to an explanation but I've told this guy more than I've told anyone else ever, so if he actually respected me then he would have told me something. Even if he didn't want to face his decision, that's just cowardly and he's still the one with the upper hand because I'm the one in the dark. I couldn't tell my mom or sister the truth because I'm tired of fucking up. It's a continuous action and I just don't want to talk about my failures with people because I feel like the closest people can get to me is always going to be at arms length.

I don't know what I said or did that made him just decide that I'm not good enough to be in his life and I don't know if it's permanent... if it's not and he comes back with some radical explanation and apology, I know I still can't trust him. I don't trust people to begin with and the fact that he somehow slipped under my strict radar pisses me off. I've learned to have feelings through the program which is why I'm more screwed up than before I entered the program because now I can't control them. I have cried every day, still away from people including family because they'd freak out thinking I was suicidal since fueled tears are new to me; it's thinking about him that makes me cry and then that familiar numbing feeling comes back. In the program the workers explained numbness to be an overwhelming amount of emotions that cannot be expressed so the mind's defense mechanism is to shut down emotion.

Was he extremely happy the last few times we were together because he knew that he was going to do this? Was this an attempt of his to hide from saying goodbye because he is leaving? Or did he plan on booting me when he left and now he's not moving? I am extremely resentful toward myself for letting someone affect me this much, to evoke emotions from me. History repeats itself repeats itself and I am so hurt and "feeling" so much that I just don't want to deal with. I know this post is very jumpy and probably not everything I wanted to say, seeing that I have a psychotic amount of obsessive thoughts brewing in my head... but this is the gist. I've learned that I cannot trust people because for some strange reason, I somehow subliminally send out a message to the best of people that they can trample on me and that it's perfectly acceptable to. I have considered that it could be his fear of getting close to people because he already warned me that he pushes people away, but this is beyond just pushing someone away (which I do too). His insecurities could have gotten the best of him, but somehow it doesn't sit well with me because I'm angry that I feel like I fucked up somewhere along the line... and don't know how to fix it for the future. No matter what, it still hurts that it's obvious that I want to talk to him more than he does to me, that I care to a point where I don't want to let him go while he sends out a foggy message to me.

I'm in pain and need advice. I sound foolish I know, and like someone who deals with these issues all the time just whining about another boy... but it's all of my other reinforced insecurities that terrifies me and makes me feel hopeless. It's like the person he is will always pop up in my life, but just with another face and name- this cycle just keeps repeating itself. It's an awful feeling to think I'm always going to be discarded, always on the outside looking in on people who know how to live. Why do people ditch me? Is it because they can have a happier life without me? It makes me sick to my stomach to think that I'm that negative of a human being.

Somewhere Out There   11-02-2006

There's not much to say here. Unfortunately people have been finding this journal online so I cannot add people as friends anymore in fear that people I know have created pseudo names just to be nosey. I think a lot of myself, huh? Bet you can't tell by my entries. Nothing is ok right now. At the end of my day I still have to live with myself and that's a struggle.

A big factor for my mood is not being on my med at all anymore, and that doesn't help with having to face the constant everyday unnecessary bullshit I have to with family and friends (unless I'm just the unnecessary bullshit, the cause of my own misery). Every time I've ever went off meds it was because I thought I was ready to but I knew I wasn't this time. Now I have 12 days to go before I can *possibly* get another type of med, meaning if I'm accepted for Social Assistance funding. It just doesn't seem to really matter to fight it anymore. Did I mention that I haven't eaten a full meal in about 4 days because of the constant nauseating feeling I have in the pit of my stomach which worsens when I eat?

Of course I'm back to serious picking again, everywhere. I almost infected a part of my hip. My face is a mess again which, is a poetically symbolic representation of my unstable moods. I'm thinking about deleting every online account I have- the ones that my real life friends can see because they don't give a shit about anything to do with me anyway. It's great to be told that because of my personality, I am not capable of loving or being loved because I push everyone away but they do the same to me because of my "*negative attitude that cannot be handled by hardly anyone*". All my insecurities coming to life!!! What a dream we all want fulfilled! I'm responsible for my own misery and it'll always be like this.

Some things I just don't want to talk about. I need to accept that I'll always have this disorder and I should just give in because fighting it really hurts me since the struggle is worth diddly- squat. Accept that no one wants to be around me and instead of dwelling on how to change that, know that I can't because I continuously get hurt when I try to. I've always been that cynical/ negative baggage that everyone wants to get a refund for... or just never pick up. I don't need anyone anyway, but my thoughts are that it would be nice to have a friend once in a blue moon.

142

A thought that raced across my mind was about lust, about intimacy. How when you read those hokey Harlequin's, the warmth of a lover's body is mentioned but it is then followed by the smoothness of a lover's skin. How hands roam an entire body and lust is heightened just by the smoothness of untainted skin, and it must be subliminal to how skin is the only thing left on a human... pure. Except obviously for me it's tainted, and it's all tainted- everything about me. Then I thought again of how hands all over my body would be like driving a car on gravel; driving on that dirt road that you dread, when instead you could really be on a paved highway with your hair flowing in the wind and a smile on your face. What exactly is appearance for a blind man? Even he could find faults in intimacy. It's not just the feel of my body, but the appearance that's clearly morphed. I look at my shoulders and upper arms in the mirror and see 2 fruit... I thought it was eggplant, but after looking at pictures it can't be that... but an unidentified fruit I see in my head but I can't place the name of it. The name eggplant is so cacophonic that should be the name of the fruit I'm trying to describe.

It's hard to ignore the obsessive nature of my thoughts, but I'm still here. I realized today that though time is the only constant in life (it never slows down or speeds up), it's easy to lose track of it. Sometimes it's easier to feel like it just stopped, to feel like time will not progress because no other areas in my life are progressing. The rare friendships I've reasoned to be the only ones I want to salvage haven't had reciprocating views. I cannot trust people because the closer I get, the further I get pushed away. I don't want to comprehend that it's my fault but after reviewing the past eight months and the very unstable friendships I have, or the ones I believed were stable out of some sick illusion that there was something normal about me somewhere, it's true. I guess that's one key to my current unhappiness- I *believed*, yet again. These ridiculous fears of abandonment issues cannot be deemed as false when it's constantly fucking happening.

In eight months: my two close friends from last year both permanently cut me off without an explanation. Three "surface" friends stopped talking to (assuming it's because I started the program), one who I am not entirely convinced that it's purely his own issues, but I'm not anticipating him contacting me again since hope doesn't do me well. It never has, and with these patterns, it is safe to assume it never will. It's not them... it's me; them versus me with an alarming ratio NOT in my favor. There's something so negative, so revolting, so plaguing about my presence and that idiotic day treatment program convinced me it was my own insecurities that need to *change*. Either way I'm never fucking trusting anyone again and I can say that whole heartedly because; there is no happiness to be let into my life and if it is it's followed by such a crash that makes it not worth trying to begin with. These feelings have wrecked me; these attempts at getting better have left me more lost and vulnerable than I can ever remember... and alone. Confined within the four walls of my apartment and still confined within the lining of my skull, yet still able to feel. I just wish I had the guts the other night because I almost did and I wish just went off the deep end. As of right now, I have no friends. I have no one to talk to, no one to listen. No one who knows. No one who cares, no one who thinks I'm worth being there for, because everyone knows I'm the lost cause that will never change. Everyone has given up on me. I'm too negative, too much of a burden, and have excess baggage, or whatever the hell you want to call it. I've fucked up on my friendships that have been worth salvaging just because I rant too much and people can't take it.

I want social functioning. I want to be allowed to care for people and to possibly be cared for- I'll add "respected" on the list later. I want to stop crying over my losses but it's all I can do when there have been no gains to replace them. And I **blame blame blame** myself for everything that has happened and how everything worth my troubles school wise, friendships, work wise has fucked up because of me, because there's something so self- sabotaging about myself. I want to want to live instead of just ending it at twenty, the year that they used to consider to be aged enough to be an antique. Antiques are supposed to be special. I want to say sorry to everyone I've brought down with me- but those chances are gone since no one ever comes back for me. I'm forgotten about or have become a distant memory engulfed with pain for those who know me the most, sadly. I've shut down completely communicatively and have no desires to share myself to people I know because there must be something about healthy human nature vs. me that doesn't rule in my favor. From reading blogs of the people who have permanently ditched me, they're doing so much better in life. Is it a facade? Probably not. Yet I am worse, so I deserve to feel like this. I just want warnings; I want people to tell me to never contact them ever again because the lingering and ambiguous pain of not knowing consumes me.

I deleted the online journal where my real life friends can read. They really don't care, they're not around, and my entries are only a mere convenience to read while they scroll down their page for updates. If they actually cared they'd contact me instead of reading any cryptic rants of apparent downfalls while still choosing to turn the other cheek. The more I write this entry the angrier I have become. Another thought- why is it when people do finally explode at me I don't reciprocate it? Instead I implode, so it's as if I get it double time. No one in my world is rooting for me and I can't blame them. I haven't felt this shitty in a long time. What's different this time is that I can feel, and that I really don't have friends around... even surface ones for me to play a social game of "House" with. I took so many fucking chances with my recovery and I knew they were risky steps, but it was all for nothing. It all amounts to today.

I want to believe that this isn't me; this is just the result of me not being on meds for about six days now. That this reaction is mostly chemical imbalances along with the already shitty life I live and how it just keeps getting oh-so-much-greater. It's just not possible to make it ok, to fix something or someone who started off broken and doomed.

Pretentious Legality Bullshit   *11-08-2006*

Tomorrow I have to prove to the province that I am worth getting the funding for having my life ruined. The woman I have to deal with wants me to bring her all of the paperwork and she has vast amounts of skepticism saying that there are many indicators that I don't qualify, with the main issue being that I have my student loan from last year which is considered to be an "asset" instead of a debt. Since it's not a student line of credit or in a separate bank account (*because we ALL know*

I saw this incompetence coming so I should have had 3 different bank accounts), it's a financial asset. These days I don't feel worth getting the money but I'm terrified if I don't. My psychiatrist appointment is on the 14th and I CANNOT get pills if I am rejected for assistance before that. If I'm rejected it'll take about a month to appeal. I feel like I don't have a month to wait for things to get better and I hate saying that and sounding melodramatic, but I really don't. The pills I need are over $100 and with no income, no balance in my bank account by the 16th when I have to pay rent... I just don't know. I'm looking forward to getting on the pill I was on 3 years ago since it was the best drug I ever tried (though I never stopped picking)... but let's face it, there's no cure. It'll always be a struggle, misinformation and lack thereof for another few decades at least. If I don't get ANYTHING for this depression and have to wait another month I just don't think I'm strong enough to fight all of this, everything.

I thought that going two and a half weeks without the pills would be tolerable. Sure I'd go through some withdrawals, down moods, but it is only for half a month, right? I almost snapped on Nov. 1st. Every few nights I'm on the verge of a breakdown induced by unnecessary bullshit going on, and then of course there are the parts of life I've always hated. I'm starting yet another grieving process of sorts and just feel like I can't handle it or everything that has led up to this useless point in my life. The flashbacks and memories, the sick things I did while during my strange episode almost two years ago... it's all built up to me not functioning on any level anymore. This semester was supposed to be taken off to become functional again. Being fucked around by a few people certainly isn't giving me strength and I'm so busy fighting with Assistance. I'm only seeing my psychiatrist once a month; so 3 therapy sessions this semester will get me up to speed? It's not even therapy- it's just a quick appointment to adjust and talk about meds. At this rate I'll be getting worse quicker than better and I'll never get out into the world. With all that's unfair in this world, why do I want to get out there? 'Cause everyone else is able to be out there? 'Cause all the cool kids are doin' it?!?!

Tonight I've been going through a lot of anxiety-related physical symptoms with the nausea and my body won't stop shaking. Is it possible that about a week and a half off the pills it's physical withdrawals or is this purely anxiety?

[EDIT]- (Next day) - I didn't submit two things so I have to go back tomorrow with that info and hopefully a decision will be made ASAP. I NEED the money and NEED the pills from Assistance. On the phone today the worker gave me flack about another bank account I can't touch plus she's lying saying she said things she didn't. Putting up with condescending bullshit or any other unnecessary pains isn't my priority. It feels like everything going on in my life could be avoided somehow and I just didn't do the best to avoid it all. Something hibernating deep down is telling me that I can't put all the blame on myself.

Shame is Close to My Name   *11-10-2006*

It doesn't look like I'm getting my new pills by the 14th. Social Assistance lied to me; not even the supervisors (yes, it's plural) would return my messages about how important it is that I get the decision made before my shrink appointment. The case worker told me to pass in the rest of the info today so it could be looked over but little did she tell me that she wouldn't be in today! Jesus Christ... I am beyond floored and they looked down on me at the office, as if I am some lazy kid just trying to work the system.

I'm so stressed out lately and feel bogged down. I don't know if what I do is wrong or right anymore, if being truthful hurts me even more, if everything bad that comes to me is my fault, etc. No one wants to deal with me and my shit but it's understandable because I have been going off the handle. I cried in front of my mom and sister over the Assistance stuff the other night. Yesterday my sister told me it was good to see me cry because I scare her with how emotionless I am. Little does she know that yes I do cry now, and yes, it's now a daily occurrence.

An embarrassing situation happened today... VERY. I was picking my skin before I left the house to go grocery shopping with my mom, and one sore on my leg was bleeding a lot. I didn't pick too deep but there was a lot of blood. So I thought I made it stop bleeding and went to the store with her. On the way home she was telling me that my face is clearing up which is good, but it's strange despite having my strings pulled and ripped out by the workers. I didn't even think of my leg because I do this all the time and I clean up before I have to leave the house. When I got home I unpacked the groceries then I sat down to relax and saw a splotch blood on my jeans the size of a dollar when I looked down.

It wasn't that bad of an opening so I don't understand why there was that much blood, but imagine how many people saw that? Not only do I wear a lot of clothing to cover my scars but it still seems to shine through another way. Something metaphorical? How I can't hide anymore? How I am powerless to all that goes wrong?

What am I going to do without meds now? I can't live like this. Not like anyone in the Assistance office cares, or anyone province except for my immediate family- and that's just because they have to. I think people need to know that they don't need to treat me like shit because I do a great enough job treating myself that way naturally.

I'm accepting defeat in many areas of my life. It's not a good feeling, but I can't change it.

Clueless 11-12-2006

I had a memory of years ago when my sister and I were having a conversation. It was about 10 years ago and she had heard that a popular celebrity wouldn't expose her legs on camera or try to mask them with movements and camera tricks. This was because when she was a teen she had dry shaved her legs really hard, which caused scarring. I remember saying back to my sister that I would hate to be in her position because my legs are the **only** physical features about myself that I liked. The shape was nice, they weren't fat, and they felt smooth.

I hope to get on meds soon, obviously. I refused to admit it until now that I have impulse problems NOT directly related to this disorder because they are non- sexual and usually when you hear about impulse control, it's either OCD- related or something sexual. Mine are different in the fact that when my thoughts race, I HAVE to do something and don't think twice about it. I've been doing more and more stupid things lately, saying stupid things, and feeling even more... stupid. It's good that I'm not going out much anymore because the last time I couldn't control my impulses was almost two years ago which was the most self-destructive time period ever for me.

I will be forcing myself to do things next semester. I'm producing the yearly one- act festival at the university, but have also been writing a play for it. I don't want it to be too dark or anything, but there are two characters in it who subtly represent my struggles of emotions vs. no emotions, and which of the two is better. I just need to work hard on it and it will be accepted because hey, I'm the producer of the show so I can be biased and put mine in somewhere. If worse comes to worse I'll cut the content down a bit. This gives me something to look forward to-something future related, even if this is so menial, superficial, and irrelevant to anything and everything.

Calling All Angels   11-18-2006

During the early morning hours of the 13th, I ODed on the last of my meds. Not to kill myself, but to numb the pain... the knowing that this is what my life has become. Lonely, empty, and trapped. To make a long story short I was in the hospital overnight, I don't remember a whole lot because I dozed in and out. By 6am I was discharged and had a severe stomach ache. I used my charm to convince the doctor that I was going to be safe until my psychiatrist appointment on the 14th. I babbled nonsense before going to the hospital, I remember. I got home ok on the bus, although every bump on the road aggravated my stomach. When I got through the door it took less than 10 minutes before I was throwing up in a bucket and my body was sweating. Not a pleasant experience; while I was popping the pills that morning, I really wanted to go into my dad's mock pharmacy and clean it out. I could have ended it and really wanted to... but I couldn't put my family through that. I was not completely out of my mind and unable comprehend the results of my actions like before. The night before this incident happened I was really upset and I was talking to my online friend. I know him in person but we've never hung out, have barely had a conversation in person, but he knows some shit about me and I was having a bad night. I hid it but he ended the conversation with something like "*You never have to be alone*". Sadly, I know have to be because I'm a burden to everyone around me. If my sister, mom, and dad gave me the ok to off myself I'd do it in a FLASH. Without hesitation, I'd kill myself.

Anyway, I got on Assistance to declare my incompetence- a shot to my pride in itself, but I'm wondering what the hell pride is anymore. I started another medication a few nights ago and it was the drug that made me the "happiest" 3 years ago. When I say happier, I mean a more tolerable state of dysphoria because I don't think I will ever live the definition of contentment. It's not mine to have and once I start to feel like I'm getting somewhere in the realm of normalcy I'm somehow knocked back down. Sometimes I don't want to go back to that because the joy seems to last for a fleeting moment, and the disappointment I face from the fall hurts me more each time.

I found out from my psychiatrist that the only therapy I'm waiting for is fucking occupational therapy. WHAT?!?!?! So I'm going to grow old on Assistance getting O.T., learning about what I want to do with my life yet not being able to do it. I'll continue to watch everyone else's lives progress and mine stay in this constant shit because anything I've ever tried to better myself has backfired, putting me in the rut I am in today. I have homework to contact the people I have pushed away and people who pushed me away. Right. A person only has so much in her before she just wants to crawl in a hole. Years of bullshit has turned me into a bitter and lonely old shrew. I've been staying offline lately because it's just not helping me and I'm too busy spiraling downward. I don't want to be hurt anymore. I don't want to be sick. I don't want these scars. I don't want to be so distant and disconnected. This med has done wonders to my body, making it hard to stay awake so hopefully I can just sleep through these miserable times and catch up with them when I'm strong enough to overcome them.

I Won't Understand Again   11-23-2006

I rarely leave the house, but today I did and caught the bus to go to the next city over. When I was about to get on the bus, the guy who tried to rape me got off and I was face to face with him for a split second. What the hell is my life- some sort of sick joke???? Out of any time to run into him, it had to be the ONE time I decide to get off my ass to go somewhere. I swear I had to have been a war criminal in my past life or something horrible and am living out the karma from that now.

Then I get on the bus and an old friend sits down beside me. She knows about my disorder, the bare minimums, meaning she doesn't understand it. We get talking and she said she picked up knitting as a new pastime. She told me it was to stop her from picking her skin and she showed me one mark on her wrist. I must have looked at her with disbelief when I asked her if it's gotten as bad as mine; she replied with a meek "no", and then looked down. I don't like when people take addictive behaviors and subconsciously belittle the severities of them just by showing a sufferer one normal trait of it. On the plus side I could have scared the shit out of her when I told her about it a while back and she wanted to do something about her normal skin picking before it got worse- if she has an addictive personality. That would be a good thing, spreading awareness so that people can prevent their lives from becoming unmanageable.

Mom is worried about me. Bobby is worried about me. He came down for the first time in a month the other day and is shocked too see how skinny I've become and how sickly I look. I know I lost weight from anxiety since I still can't eat a whole lot, plus I keep having diarrhea every day. Mom jokingly called me anorexic yesterday but I didn't think it was funny, especially because she was trying to shove any food into me 2 nights ago and I told her to leave me alone because I wasn't hungry. The other day I bought some multi-vitamins so that I can look somewhat healthy and go out into public without looking like some sort of drug addict. When I get my check at the end of the month I will probably venture off to find some Vitamin E oil to speed up the healing process of my skin, like I read in an online forum.

I'm still hurting and feeling abandoned, more so than ever since my ping pong buddy, Tony, has only sent me one e-mail in a month and a half and blocked me from IMing. I just want things to be ok. I don't want people to toss me out like the fucking trash I feel like I am. It's still surreal to me because I should have seen it coming- it's what always happens. I really miss being with someone who understands more than the superficial elements of life and someone who I can feel ok to be myself around. I miss him and hate it; I despise having someone affect me so deeply since it's rare that anyone does. I just have to always keep it in the back of my mind that people hurt people- simple as that.

Sick Coincidence   11-23-2006

I saw that asshole AGAIN today. At first he wasn't going to catch the bus I was on, but just as the bus was pulling away he ran to catch it and got on. Not just that but I could feel him peering down at me and there were SO many empty seats but he sat directly in front of me. I wish he would go kill himself or die slowly so that I could feel safer; I would then spit on his grave for closure. I felt trapped because I was sitting in the very back corner and no one else was around us. Twice within five days... I REALLY must have been a shit disturber in a past life. I was on the bus with him for a maximum of 15 minutes but I made sure not to make any eye contact with him… or hurt and scar HIM like he has to me.

Other than that I've been feeling great lately and things have done a complete 180, which is why I'm even more pissed off because of the above mentioned. I've been leaving the house more and I swear it has to be the meds kicking in. I have plans for this week and the daily grind of negativity just isn't bogging me down. Another bonus is that my impulsive behavior (*other than the picking, of course*) has gone away for the most part and I haven't felt this confident in a long while. My obsessive thoughts have slowed down significantly, although they're always going to be there. I'm not hoping every day that death will come to me and I'm not planning the hundreds of ways I can make it happen. I was very sick and still am but not nearly as much as I was. I hope this motivation lasts a while but it must be chemically induced since nothing in my life has changed for the better ***except*** for my mood.

The Girl That Everybody Leaves Behind...   12-13-2006

There is much to write, but I'll try to keep the content minimal because I'm only writing out of boredom while I try to download something for the computer. First of all, I'm glad that I came out of that really rough spot a few weeks ago. Looking back I can see just how sick my mind was, primarily because in those three weeks I cried every single day and some days, more than once. The thing about crying is I do it now when I get upset; it's so automatic and I wish I could shut it off like I could before. Maybe it's a sign of improvement to cry, or I just want to tell myself that because everyone else says it's healthy.

I didn't go to the Theatre Formal this semester. Case in point, it was because my shoulders and upper chest are certainly much worse than last year. It's funny how I look back a year ago and how I knew this disorder was out of control, yet I convinced myself that I was in control of it because I would do it ONLY to my legs, back, and sometimes my face. Denial. All of my fancy formal-like outfits reveal my shoulders; although I know it wouldn't be a big deal to people around me I know that I would be extremely anxious knowing that people could see my scars because I know how they got there. Really, it doesn't matter what other people think or say but I'm ashamed of how I have no power over this.

Four days ago I told myself that I should try to stop picking since my moods are more consistent. I can tell they're not completely controlled because when anything unpleasant happens I go into a slump for the rest of the night. As I sit in front of the bathroom mirror, I pick my face while telling myself that I shouldn't do it... instead of acknowledging ASAP that I AM doing it. I don't want to abruptly stop picking but reduce it because I know around Christmas the cameras will come out and I can't dodge them throughout the holidays. Three days ago I ended up really tearing a strip out of my chin and it now resembles a cigarette burn. What made me decide to try and quit again is because of something about a week ago that happened when I was awake early and on my computer. I got up a few times and walked around, making failed attempts of making my room a bit more organized. When I went to the bathroom to engage in my routines, I saw a lot of blood on the floor and didn't know where it came from. Then I noticed it was from my baby toe. After retracing my steps I saw a trail of blood in the hallway, kitchen, a few dots in my parents' room, and some blotched spots in my room. It looked like I cut my toe, not picked it; I know my skin is desensitized to cuts/ scrapes/ picks so I don't notice when I hurt myself and end up making a bloody mess (literally). I still need to carpet clean my room but it's probably stained now and if anyone comes into my room how will I explain that one?

I've become nocturnal. I wake up anywhere between 5pm and 8pm, then go to sleep around 10am. It's more tranquil to stay away and only hear the hum of the computer, play with my cat, and not have to hear constant nagging. Is it avoidance? I think so but I want to feel relaxed before I try to do life- stuff again. I don't want to cry in front of people and I cry so frequently at any emotional disturbance that I can't control the waterworks... and it's embarrassing. With my picking, I am still going to make a conscious effort, as much as possible, to reduce it. My face looked a bit better until two days ago... and yesterday... when I went at it intensely. I was very grouchy and agitated, so it helped calm me down. I don't feel so lost and powerless, even if in reality I truly am powerless.

- CHAPTER IV Giving It All I Have -

Express Yourself   *12-17-2006*

I finally learned this summer that, yes, I do have a womanly shape. I don't have the body of a twelve year old. I learned this through some self-acceptance. I haven't exercised in about a month so my stomach isn't entirely in shape, but instead of always hating myself for my scars I should be content with the shape of my body. I plan on exercising again because I'll be taking a dance course next semester and want to be in shape for it.

I seem to be slipping a bit again with my moods. I swear I've become immune to this dose of meds, which then causes my thoughts to start racing. On the 21st my pill will be upped again to the maximum dose, so hopefully there will be a mood boost sometime after that. I can't believe the mess that I was in a little over a month ago, how damn low I got. I'm torn about the new year- very torn. I'm producing a festival and am supposed to be writing one of the one-act plays in it, but I'm not sure if I'm up to the task. I need to force myself to be social again, or at least do **something**. I've procrastinated far too much about the play I'm writing and barely have a start on it, but I want this to be an accomplishment. I need to believe in myself.

Acting? Not doing that in the near future. After watching two plays last month, I just can't see myself onstage with the scars on my face exposed. I'm now more self-conscious than before in that respect and get too distressed with trying to hide the new messes and the old.

This entry isn't an intellectual one. I tired myself out earlier today with multiple debates and an in-depth conversation with a friend of mine. Instead, this entry is marked as verbal vomit. One of my dear friends picked up some Vitamin E oil for me so I need to get it from her soon if I want to look half decent for Christmas. Christmas= cameras= pictures of me. I don't want to be so embarrassed of them that when my mom's not watching I'll delete them from her camera or folder on the computer like I have many times before. "Oops"! I don't particularly like my appearance but I can live with it- I just don't want to have another year, marked in history by a camera, showing everyone my self-terrorism.

Should I Run, Should I Hide?   *12-24-2006*

So, technically it's Christmas Eve and I'm miserable. Miserable for even *feeling* miserable; it's quite the cycle, I must say. I've never been one to trust emotions since they undermine logic and overbear the mind when it comes to decision making. Right now is a perfect example of this because I know I have lots to be thankful for, yet I feel trapped within myself and overwhelmed by everything that's wrong with life- everything that's wrong with me. How is it that I push my friends and family away, yet complain that I am alone? It must be because I have that teenage-angst mindset of being misunderstood and forgotten. I become more afraid of getting close to people as time moves on, yet there's that part inside of me that still strives to connect with someone because it quenches my thirst of feeling normal. My two old friends that were a couple, and Tony, were all awesome to me during our interactions but I think that if I knew what the future would have held, I wouldn't have made myself emotionally vulnerable to them.

Taking a look at everything that has happened just in this year is terrifying for me. It involved little stress in comparison to other years but the drama it created has exasperated my mind because I can't handle it anymore. It seems that any effort I put into something I trust and believe in, I'm beaten repeatedly like a dead horse. I'm so tired now and believing the best in people is what hurts me the most when **they let me down**. I don't ask for much- just for the ability to move on. The female in the couple (Jennifer) made up shit about me in her own head and ended up believing it to make herself feel better about her very drastic lifestyle changes and the male (Ned) loves her, so it's obvious where his loyalty lies. Tony knew about how those friendships affected me. Every day I beat myself up over the fact that I actually fell for Tony because I should have avoided it. I felt that my feelings were safe with him since they were only emotions and that were never going to be acted upon. I think he decided to chop me out of his life abruptly because I was too annoying, talkative, wanting, and negative. Now I'm the one left to wonder, I'm the one left to scrounge around and find ways to sort out feelings of anger, understanding, patience, and confusion. It wouldn't have taken me long to get over that fuzzy feeling for him, but I was content with only a friendship. In many ways, I'd probably be happier because a relation on a deeper level scares me more than it should. I'm a sucker for punishment because I would still love to be his friend- under the premise that it was his issues that were overwhelming, and had nothing to do with me specifically.

In these three cases, I feel like the piece of shit. It's times like these where I wish that people respected me. Specifically, people who I respect[ed] because I don't care about what people I DON'T respect on an interpersonal level think. I guess I trusted them all with my feelings and it backfired every. damned. time. Each blow seems to have taken a part of my spirit and I dwell on it more than the average person because I already went into each friendship damaged. I knew that if anything had happened between Jennifer and I or Ned and I that the other one would immediately take the other's back because they were a couple... but I was too naive to see the possibility of anything happening. Without going into details, I knew that Tony knew what abandonment felt like so therefore I thought that he would never do it to anyone. But they say that this is how vicious cycles begin. Another friend from the program explained to me her theory saying that when people are hurt they almost accept it as a way of life and feel that THEY were weak to hurt over it. So then, they do it to other people just because they want to believe that their pain is justified.

I miss the 3 of them. I have more hostility toward Jennifer and a bit of anger with pity for Ned, but with Tony it's so damn confusing. I'm nothing to him, not worth an explanation, not worth having peace of mind, so I should take that and run instead of dwell on it. In time I will internalize that I was a moron for thinking that I can have a close and stable friendship. I hold hatred toward myself for missing these people when they clearly don't miss me, or not enough to want to be near me. I don't understand how I'm plaguing to other people unless it's because I'm so plaguing to myself. I'd rather not be in my own presence because of my terminal negativity and views but I'm stuck with me- everyone else has an option.

With that out of the way, I asked my close friend to pick up some Vitamin E oil for me. She works at a drug store and gets discounts so I was going to pay her back. She knows that it's for what I do to my skin, but I am unable to communicate the exact distress and repercussions this disorder does to me. Anyway, we exchanged Christmas gifts the other day and she gave that to me too and insisted that I not pay her back for it. It's pretty expensive and I felt horrible but she kept saying it was a part of the present. It was a very sweet and touching gesture but I couldn't show her, for some reason, how much I appreciated her reaching out to me.

I have been putting the oil on my face for a few days now and it's helping in the sense that it's harder to pick, but my face is an absolute wreck. My psychiatrist made a note of saying that the other day when I went to see her. Three weeks before my last appointment I was worried about my anxiety, so she took my weight- 138Lbs. Since then my anxiety has worsened and I'm nauseous all the time. Anything I eat or drink causes me to have severe diarrhea (going an average of 4 times within the first 2 hours I wake up). She then checked my weight the other day and I am now at 131Lbs. She's also concerned and I'm frustrated with all of this. She wants me to get tests done to make sure it's not a GI infection but I really don't think it is. Tonight for example, my mom made a really yummy supper of chicken, sour cream n' chives potatoes, and cream corn. I love it all but I was only able to eat about 1/4th of it, which included one bite of the chicken and I had to leave the table; I thought I was going to throw up so I had to go lie down for a few hours. My eating habits for Christmas dinner won't change since I barely eat for major dinners since elementary school because I was made fun of by relatives for being chubby... so I don't do it anymore. My psychiatrist said that with all the fluids I'm losing so rapidly that if it's still decreasing at this rate I could end up in emergency room in a few weeks. I doubt it because I'm trying to drink a lot of fluids, but this is just a severe annoyance. I love my food! My psychiatrist is worried that the pill could be contributing to this so she won't raise my dosage for a little bit, but I care more about my mentality than my physical health. I am worried that I lost 5% of my body weight in such little time and what mental stability I have left could be compromised because of this issue. She also informed me that the average weight for a woman my height and age is between 145Lbs and 160Lbs.

I needed a new focus, so I got it. Three days ago I got my ear pierced with a piercing called an "Industrial". It'll keep my mind fixated on something else other than my current shitty way of life. I was very upset the other day with my appointment, with a new psychologist who I'll call Dr. A. To put it bluntly, she's a bitch. Within ten minutes she said I was a "*cold, distant, angry young woman*". Thanks. I know she's telling me how it is, BUT, a few times I felt like she was implicating me as a liar about things. It continued like this throughout the whole session and by the end of it I told her that it felt like she didn't like my personality and she completely dodged that accusation with something stupid. I cried within five minutes of being in the room with her because it was so intimidating, even before it got to big questions. It's a strange reaction because when I was questioned in the program, I didn't cry but now I'm so emotionally unstable, and talking about the past is truly overwhelming. Near the end of the evaluation it felt surreal- like we were fictitious and in some sort of surreal thriller movie. She looked more 2D and it scared me; her stares felt like the pause button was hit. When I left I coincidentally ran into someone from the program that also was leaving an appointment. The moment I hugged her I started crying again but it was nice to see her because I knew immediately that she understood. She walked me to the bus stop and in the little time we had I felt like I completely non- verbally updated her. Well, with only a few words.

Sorry for the long entry. Read it all if you want. If not, it's all good. I just needed to get it all out of me. I'm just so damn tempted from tomorrow on to hide in my room and play my RPG's until the New Year, when the celebrations of other people's fortunate lives are over. I have plans for the New Year with dance class and the festival I'm producing but until then, I'm scared about my health and scared about the decisions I have to make in the future. Who I should trust?

Countin' all the Reasons Why   01-01-2007

Looking back on 2006 is painful, but it really shouldn't be since my worst year was 2005 and I didn't react this badly. Being in that program was one of the worst choices I ever made, but I was desperate to feel better about myself and the world around me. I began to trust people and as much as I'd like to say that I'm an open person, I'm also very private. I warmed up to people and I displayed histrionics in my emotions that surprised me. No longer can I get sarcastic and suck it up when people hurt me; I cry and can't rebut, or I completely shut down.

I never expected my year to be like this: Losing so many people, having people pulling my strings more than ever in my social life. I had false dreams of becoming an actress only because I wanted to defy my illness. I wanted to prove something to myself- that I could be anything. Despite my scars, I would get around makeup and costuming somehow... with faith. So much of my life has been a fucking lie and when I'm honest with myself, I crash.

I got stoned last night for the first time in seven months. I came home and ripped my face apart, despite my eyelids shutting every few seconds. I didn't feel stoned though... I felt more stoned in November off of my meds than last night. I tried to get plastered on Boxing Day which was also a flop; somehow I'm nearly immune to all of it and I shouldn't be. I slept through as much of Christmas as my family let me, both Eve and Day. When I had to come out and visit with my relatives, I tried to remain a background figure. The house was coincidentally fuller than it's ever been and I was put on the spot a few times. Near the end of my aunt and uncle's visit my aunt asked about my tattoos and piercings. My sister's friend didn't know about my wing tattoos and everyone wanted to see them. My sister pushed me into her room with four other people going into the room so I could lift up my shirt and have them see. I quickly whispered to my sister I don't want to because of my scars but she said "it's ok". I couldn't think of a lame excuse to get out of it and I was terrified of being exposed.

166

Afterward, my aunt came up to me and asked me, "*Why in the world would you go and mutilate your beautiful body?*" and I almost shit myself. Luckily, not literally with the way my stomach is being. I thought she was talking about my scars, which to me looked better that day, but they're still disgusting. My sister's friend started to take out her camera and I absolutely refused to have a picture taken of them. For a little bit, the website for the shop I got it done at had it on their webpage... and then I noticed that my picture was the only one removed. With everyone in the living room after, I was chewed out for about 20 minutes and I was able to keep my apathetic demeanor but I was boiling inside. I refused to get my picture taken because I'm severely insecure, but I got stuck in two. I was put on the spot about school and how it's going. I answer the same way every time, "It's going", while a chunk of the room knows that I haven't been in school all semester. I said it's not bad and I don't know how long I'll have but I'm taking it slow.

I got a gift card from them for $25CDN and am considering buying a bottle of Vitamin E oil for when mine runs out, which was been quicker than I'd like. Maybe buy two bottles or one bottle of oil and a container of multi-vitamins. The oil helps the healing process better than nothing would.

I don't know if I'm still losing weight, but I've been eating better since my dosage went up. Meaning, I'm actually eating now. The physical side effects to anxiety have been gone since the last entry except for one day when I was very upset. Since I used to be made fun of for my chubbiness when I was a kid, a sick part of me does like this weight loss... maybe because it somehow makes up for when I was powerless to my body as a kid. I don't have an eating disorder but I do fear gaining weight. I can't recall a time when I ever admitted that I like losing weight to anyone. I know I'm not fat, or chubby, and can see I'm skinnier than I should be and a few more pounds would balance my proportions, but there's a small voice inside of me saying that I'm better off withering away.

This year I'm moving out alone by September at the latest. Through the years, shrinks have told both me and my sister it's very difficult to get better in our stressful environment. My dad with his brain injury gets downright neurotic and repetitive; meanwhile, my mom will not admit to her flaws which are what I think I need to connect with her on a personal level. She again called me cold the other day because my cousin made my sister a homemade stitched picture that has a bunny on it and says something warm and I mentioned how it was weird that my cousin told me that she didn't know what to make me because I thought that she'd make me something similar. My mom said I'm a cold fish and people are scared to give me things filled with compassion. Then she said she doesn't understand why I am the way I am since she raised me differently. I think I can guess why I am this way, but it's too long of an entry anyway now. I may even move to a sublet in April or May, but no roommates because I'm a secluded person and also, I need to think of the time I spend in the bathroom, how I wouldn't be able to roam freely in my own home wearing shorts, etc. I found a bachelor's apartment for $610 which already includes heat and wireless internet. It's near my university, the building I went to the rehab to, and a short bus ride to see Dr. A.

When I move out though, I know I won't go home often and my mom will subconsciously make me feel unwelcome with visiting. I fear that, and I fear that if I run out of money I'll have nowhere to go since I won't be allowed to return, due to their financial situation. But I do feel trapped here, in this city, in my home, without any room to breathe and grow. I can't imagine living here for another full year. Even September seems to be a lifetime away.

Anyway, this year **will** be different. I don't know if it will benefit me or not, but things in the program that were taught to us were taught to us under the basis that life is a controlled substance. Then we were thrown back into our old lives without knowing how to deal with old memories and the feelings accompanying them. But yes, this will be different because I need to go back in time a bit and adapt to parts of my pre-program self. I will regain my control and ability to smile when I only want to crawl into a hole. No one will get the best of me again. Life, for some reason, just isn't what the program advertised that mine could be. Is it my fault? Did I fail at executing everything they showed me? My life isn't easily molded to perfection.

Hate's All the World's Ever Seen   *01-18-2007*

I've been trying to keep busy with the festival that I'm producing, which has been far more successful than imagined thus far. The auditions were 110% full on the two nights we were holding them. Everyone has been cast, but we still need to find a room to perform in. I've been thinking about writing/ performing a monologue, revealing my scars and having it involve me doing soliloquy about how appearances are irrelevant in the grand scheme of things. I'm obviously hesitant but also reluctant because, to me, it's almost a cheap way of displaying or humiliating myself just for the sake of in-depth and moving theatre. On the other hand, it could be opening up to strangers about another lifestyle that they would not regularly be accustomed to. I'm torn and most likely not going to do it, but it's a passing thought... especially since this festival is run by me.

I could not have done this festival last semester with the way I was thinking. If I stay feeling structured like this for a long time, I would be lucky because I can compare it to how I've felt in the past. It doesn't make the anxiety disappear or lessen the picking, but I can attempt to lead a mediocre life without being completely housebound.

I went to see my psychiatrist today, well... technically yesterday. I have a date on Valentine's Day with her, of course, haha. I enjoy those visits probably more than I should; it was freezing outside today and as I was about to leave she noticed that my jacket could be adjusted and like a mom, she toyed with the strings on my jacket for me. For some reason, that felt nice although it made no difference going outside. I mean, something so superficial grabbed her attention and she wanted me to be more comfortable. Surprisingly I lost three pounds because of the constant diarrhea, which brings me down to 128Lbs. The diarrhea had slowed down before Christmas I but came back 6 days ago. That tiny piece of destruction inside of me is thriving off this damage from remembering when I was pudgy years ago and how I was teased... how I wanted to look like this. No, not look like **this**, but have my body shape be the norm so that I could be relieved of ridicule. I don't want to weigh anything over 140lbs, but I think my ideal weight that I would be 135lbs. My moods are relatively stable as emotions are quieting down and becoming numb. Is this a good thing or does this mean that I'm "hiding" from my feelings again? How does one differentiate healing from hiding? I see Dr. A tomorrow (Friday afternoon) for my 2nd appointment; it should be a BLAST *rolls eyes*. She cancelled on me twice already so her reliability is getting increasingly sketchy... although my lack of fondness for her could add to that!

To bed I go now... before I fall asleep on the floor.

Pain's the Name of the Game 01-22-2008

Like I predicted, part 2 of Dr. A's assessment did not benefit me at all. So much has been swirling in my mind since the last appointment but overall I feel like a rotten piece of shit. I'll try to break it down in a coherent fashion but it may not be that easy.

First, we had a little spat about what a therapist/ patient relationship is like. I told her that I don't know what it's *supposed* to be and she said it's professional. I told her that when I hear "professionalism" used in this context, I believe that I have to reflect the same demeanor back. Then, Dr. A said that there is a trust, but not a friendship because she does not want to be my friend. She kept asking me if I could trust her because I'm very skeptical, and that she would continue if I warmed up to her; she also confessed that I'm so aloof that it'll take longer than usual to help me. Keep in mind that in the 1st appointment with her she accused me of not trying to help myself because *"With all of the therapy you've received, you've gotten worse over the years.*

So you're saying that these people couldn't help you?" and she continued to imply that I haven't tried.

Oh, and apparently the way I speak to people is not becoming of my character (my interpretation). She said though that if she spoke to me in the cold way that I speak to her that I would be annoyed with her. She then asked me to use words to negatively describe myself. I replied, "*Cold, distant, ugly, cynical, picking my skin doesn't help*" and she was satisfied with that answer. Then she asked me to describe myself positively and I said "*trustworthy, honest, insightful, and funny*". When she heard me say funny, her robotic tone lost its monotony and she exclaimed, "*You, FUNNY?*' I was really miffed by that and I asked why she was surprised and she simply stated that I just don't seem to be funny. DUH- I'm not in therapy to crack jokes. She then proceeded to pick apart my "honesty" description by saying that I'm too honest and how it's a defense mechanism since I show no emotion; she also explained that I tell people things they don't want to hear to piss them off so that they'll distance themselves from me. To a point she's right because I am too blunt sometimes, but she made it sound like I vindictively plot to hurt people to gain satisfaction. Finally, she asked me a question that I forget now what it was and I answered with "I don't know", which she responded to by saying that she can't fathom how someone who says she's insightful does not know the answer.

So she tore apart every positive adjective, except one, and ended up nodding her head to all the negative terms. I don't want to quit therapy because maybe this is how to get better; maybe it'll work out in the long run so I can see the bad in myself and change it. I don't know. I don't know anything. Maybe she's doing this to provoke me but I'm not even thinking she likes me- at all. I'm now questioning myself as a person regarding how cold others perceive me and how my inability to socially mesh growing up was completely my own doing. Maybe it wasn't that people looked down on me for not being like them or intolerant, but maybe I was snub- nosed and no one could put up with that part of me. No one gets close to me, on any level, because they start to see the true me and back out when necessary. It makes so much sense how so many people have been in the revolving door of friendship with me unless they don't get close enough to know the true me.

I don't purposely hurt people. The way that Dr. A described how people see me is daunting. I really feel like I fucked up as a kid and grew up to be rotten. I'm not even really shaken by this emotionally- it's just in my head but it's not helping to change my moods.

In conclusion, she said that my skin picking WILL STOP when I am able to sort through issues from my past along with some lingering ones. That's what the professionals in the program said this summer and it actually worsened my skin picking. I tried explaining that to her but she said that I'm being stubborn and don't believe that I have the power to stop this, so I won't. What she said overwhelmed me because a disorder just doesn't disappear- a disorder is developed, yes, due to past circumstances, but it doesn't mean that when those are talked through, the disorder disappears. I feel like I'm going in circles and wasting my time by being degraded and ridiculed. I hope that this is just a strategy to make me recognize my flaws to provoke a start to the changing process. I'm going back because if I don't I'll chance losing my disability funding, but more egotistically important to me it's as if she wins... she wins in thinking that I'm close-minded, not trying, am too cynical, etc. Maybe that's a strategy too though. I wish I knew something.

Interview– Like   01-29-2007

Maybe you have wondered a few things about me that don't make sense; that I just bitch and moan but do nothing to change my life, especially when it comes to skin picking. Word-for-word, I thought I'd try my best to clear up a bit of confusion with some questions someone bombarded me with.

(1) "The program wasn't much of anything as far as I'm concerned. Every time you talk about whether or not the skin picking will stop you go back to the 'intervention' and remind yourself how much worse it got. You can't base the extent of your abilities on what you learned from one little chapter of your life."

It irks me that when I first came into the program, it was far from what I expected. They didn't take the disorder seriously because they thought it was more me "acting out" and if I worked through my problems, I wouldn't have to pick anymore.

(2) "I have to say, and I know you won't like this, but I have to agree that it is something that could stop."

Maybe it can stop. I don't know. No one knows. The urges will never go away and life will be a struggle fighting the urges whether or not I give in. Even if something miraculous were to happen, like some new treatment to turn this around, the urges are hell.

(3) *"If you had to pick one answer would you say you enjoy it or hate it?"*

I **can't** pick one answer. Maybe it's unfathomable for you to comprehend, but it's impossible. With any addiction, giving into the urge is more of a relief than what can be found elsewhere. My problems become more manageable, more controlled... like my emotions. Occupying myself with game consoles, online, socializing, dancing... nothing gives me the satisfaction/ rejuvenation of just losing myself in a picking session. I enjoy the way it makes me feel but despise the messy aftermath and addictive nature of it.

(4) *"If someone were to chop off your hands and stick you in an environment where you COULDN'T pick, first you'd probably cry a whole lot, then the urge would drive you ballistic and then eventually you'd give up on picking because it wouldn't be worth the struggle."*

The urge grows stronger and stronger; without the reactive behavior, I can't even function. Being ballistic is not what I want because I need to keep some form of composure to be able to tend to responsibilities in all areas of my life. The chaos is the disorder, but in order to gain some success I need to find an alternative way so that my life doesn't break out in a similar chaos.

(5) *"So quit trying to pass the responsibility on to someone else, nobody wants it, it's yours. So what is it you really really want?"*

The first sentence was severely harsh and I hope I'm misinterpreting the meaning of it. What I REALLY want is to never have the urges again, then never pick, and then my self-confidence would be higher.

(6) *"You're probably likening me to all those other people who just don't understand how hard it is for you. But I do care. A whole lot. And I would like to see someday that you've been able to get over it and devote all that time and energy towards more beneficial things."*

To an extent, yes I am. There's a reason why no real life friends can see this journal. If they really knew the intensity of the way I think, then they'd give me this same speech like they have about my general depression. That makes me not trust people enough to talk about this disorder.

(7) *"But I don't get why you think about it so much, why you have a journal devoted solely to your struggles with it."*

First, I made this journal to find people who have this disorder like I do to relate to them and not feel alone. I need to get thoughts off of my chest but I do not want my real- life friends to read it so candidly. If you've noticed, many paragraphs are also focused on other matters in my life.

These comments really didn't help me when I was feeling especially down about my session[s] with Dr. A. I've been avoiding replying because I hate having to justify myself because most people just aren't worth the breath. I feel like I'm constantly being betrayed by people so I'm ultra- sensitive to ridicule, or even the controversial "tough love" approach. It's hard to describe the hopelessness I feel some days when I haven't heard of a success story of anyone in this situation plus there aren't any guaranteed treatments... or any that bring the urges to a halt. I feel angrier at myself and I want to give myself that "of course I can do it" attitude, but how can I give up an essential part of my without anything to replace it with? Nothing that gives me as much stability, anyway.

A Burning in my Pride   02-17-2007

After seeing two recent self-portraits of me, I can't even relate to them. Especially in the photo shopped pictures because I look kind of gross; I seem to lose the weight in all the wrong places.

Speaking of the weight, I had an appointment with Dr. W three days ago. When she saw me she immediately asked if I lost weight, and I thought I gained some. I lost two more pounds in a 3-4 week span so it isn't a drastic hike like before. She told it looks like I'm disappearing. To put it politely, my "stomach issues" have calmed down a lot so I don't know where the weight loss is from. It scares me that I don't think these pictures look a thing like me. I've always been tummy shy, but these pictures compliment my stomach... I don't get it.

Had my Dr. A appointment yesterday. She pissed me off extremely but I know she wants to get me visibly angry. After saying something aggravating she'd ask, "*How would I know you're angry? You're sitting there all calm and serene*". She's still on her kick that I'm an arrogant person, but get this. THIS is what really pisses me off. Although I've been picking my whole life, she says that I made up a unique way of hurting myself because I want to be different. That I think I'm superior to everyone else; also, that I resent every one of my friends which is why

I don't hang out with them. Reverting back to the picking, I said that it's something I've done my whole life and it only got worse when I was 13. She said, "*well, maybe you've been needy of attention your whole life*". I mentioned that I don't drink nor do I cut my skin so I didn't think this would be addicting and she said I don't do the first two actions because I think I'm better than everyone else. For a disorder with **many** theories, she's quick to jump on that one and not even think that it's a compilation of factors; for a disorder without a whole lot of information on it she seems to be convinced everything's my fault... consciously. I know I get defensively arrogant but the second part is downright untrue. I kept this a secret from EVERYONE for 5 years except for my family and my now ex-boyfriend. How is that being histrionic?

The only thing that keeps me returning to Dr. A is that a part of me thinks that I need a hardcore bitch of a therapist who can provoke emotions from me because for the last 10 years, I've felt nothing with others. We were also digging into why I don't leave the house often. Again she took out her blaming pistols, but I know I'm not there to be praised on what's perceived as "good" about me. I'm there to recognize the bad and work on it. I have many socializing plans this week and I am going to go through with them because something in me feels more confident- so maybe there is going to be good coming out of this. In the meantime, I just hate feeling like the world's most rotten person who ever existed.

Sometimes I wonder sometimes if she's taking this approach because of the bad rap that people with Borderline Personality Disorder have: the whole manipulative, sneaky, malice, behavior stigma. Overall I think she's trying to get me to show her how I'm feeling instead of being a stone and using my head to talk about my issues. I'm still not convinced that feeling emotions are constructive experiences in the long run but maybe showing them makes me look more human by removing my stand- offish demeanor and help my relationships. Who knows?

I'll Make You What I Never Was　　　　　*03-13-2007*

It's been awhile. I've been extremely busy with the show I'm producing, and yes acting in. Specifically I'm doing a monologue about scars and body image, meaning my scars will be shown onstage. Is it a cheap tactic in getting an audience's reaction? Perhaps. My current problem is that I have to have my monologue memorized by the 29th... 12 days from now because that's the tech run. A darker cloud looming over my head is that I have to actually WRITE the damn thing. I have it playing in my head over and over with subtle variations each time, but I need something concrete for the stage manager to have lighting cues. I need a hint of self- discipline to get a head start; although I've winged it with other shows by memorizing two days before show time, this monologue is something [*that's going to be*] written by me... something very personal. I don't want this monologue to just be winged- I want it to be mesmerizing. I'm busy until show time with ticket selling and various preparations, appointments, and obligations. Tonight I'm forcing myself to write this up, even if I've said that now for the last 6 nights...

Performances= March 30th & 31st. I still wonder if I'm in my right mind going through with this. My monologue will be called, "*Blinded by Sight*". I hope to get feedback about my absurd plan of going through with this!

With that somewhat of out of the way, yesterday I weighed in at 124lbs. For the last week and a half my anxiety has gone through the roof. I haven't been sleeping well, have had massive diarrhea, that anxious/ heavy feeling in the heart, and some nausea. Dr. W won't give me an anti-anxiety pill for it because she said I have an addictive personality and in a time like now when I really need it I'll become dependent on it. Instead, she gave me a sedative that has a mild anti-depressant component to it. I took one at 10:30pm last night and was out cold a little after midnight.

I'm pleased to report that my arms have been healing rather well, my upper chest continues to recover, and my face is less picked at. I had a major confidence booster the other day when I dyed my hair red. Hopefully it'll still be vibrant for when I'm onstage. What's really silly is that my scars will be shown onstage, but I want my face to be clear by the show. God, that's so contradictory! Maybe it's because I strive for my face to show improvements because my legs are damaged for life.

Monologue   *03-25-2007*

The setting is in a bedroom. A girl is getting ready to socialize when a friend comes to her door and informs her of some plan changes...

* Sings and puts on makeup *

Oh! Don't scare me like that! Can't you knock before coming in?!?!?!

Anyway, so the party is... where exactly? What? Why did the plans change again?

upset *I'm not going to the beach. Well... really,* IT'S THAT TIME OF MONTH AGAIN.

Okay, okay, so I've been saying that all summer... BUT...

Are you calling me insecure? C'mon now, look at me! I'm one hell of a sexy bitch!

...Actually... I guess you'd be partially correct. I mean, everyone is self- conscious to an extent, right? People say, "I'm too fat" or "I'm too skinny", "I'm too tall" or "I'm too short" and the list goes on. It's ridiculous how people judge other people on their looks and judge themselves because they fear rejection based on not looking a certain way. <u>Seriously</u>, just imagine if no one was born with sight. Just close your eyes for a few minutes and think how different things would be.

* Lights out completely *

Hi! How are you today?

See... you wouldn't have to worry about presenting yourself in an acceptable way. Rather, you could look like shit and no one would care, though you would still need to be hygienic or else you would stink... aaaand you'd have to watch more carefully what you say....

Why take away our sight anyway? It really wouldn't fix a first impression. What if our *speaks low* "voices sounded like this"-- then we'd still be ridiculed! By taking away our sight we'd be missing out on so much that nature has to offer us. We

181

wouldn't fully experience what it's like to watch the sun set with a loved one, or to wake up and see the first snowfall of the year.

The only advantage of taking away our sight is that we would have to be heard. Our minds are what would be paid attention to instead of whether or not we have A- cups or double D's. If we all listened to each other more, we'd be more informed and more enriched by our social interactions.

The real question is WHY can't we love ourselves? WHY can't we accept the only person who will remain in our lives forever?

* Lights back on. Is handcuffed to her chair, wearing a bikini that shows her scars *

Because we want perfection. WE are our own worst critic when we should be our own best friend. We all see these similar images of what beauty is to the majority of the public and WE want to amount to that. And why not? No one wants to settle for second best, so instead we choose to go to ANY measures to reach that ultimate goal.

picks up mirror and aims to audience What do you see here?

Ok... I see how your nose turns up as you examine yourself head to toe. What don't you like about yourself? Seriously?

.

So... do you think that just because you have a healthy amount of body fat that it makes you less of a person? I can't even get over how absurd the human condition is... even though I'm part of it. Who cares if you have a little bump on your nose? If no one had distinguishing physical characteristics, then we'd all be the same. We wouldn't be given the chance to even open our minds to learn from others.

182

But beauty isn't about appearance. It's <u>truly</u> about how you view yourself and what kind of genuine confidence you have IN yourself. It doesn't matter how hard anyone fakes it, if you don't like yourself... everyone can see that. What employer would want to hire someone who carries this deadweight when they can hire someone radiant, someone who is confident in every action she takes?

I want to wake up and sigh in relief to know that it's ok to be me because if I was any different, I just wouldn't be who I want to be. But what if we all turned around our insecurities and even loved ourselves? Think what the world would be like.

{*Finally gets handcuffs off*}

Then what we would see is everyone smiling around us. To me, that is a sight that I wouldn't want to miss out on.

- END –

I have to have it memorized for the 29th, which is tech rehearsal day. I know once it hits me that, yes, I'm going onstage... I'll freak out. I've been panicking already about getting the show together by staying up to date with directors, funds, printing, etc. Unconventionally, I've been listening to myself recorded over and over to memorize lines instead of just reading the script I wrote. I pressed the "repeat" button before I went to sleep in hopes that my subconscious will pick up on lines... and it has really helped, especially because I'm an auditory learner. The recording is 5:05 in total, but with onstage blocking the performance should be approximately 10 minutes long.

The script itself isn't about Dermatillomania; it's about body image and appearance. There will be a chair onstage the whole time and at the beginning I lug around the chair and it looks casual but when the lights come back on and my foot is handcuffed to the chair, it takes on a symbolic meaning while I try to hide it and escape from it.

Tomorrow or the next day I'm going to find an empty apartment in my building (*by asking the superintendent, NOT by barging in*!) so I can fully act it out. It's embarrassing to do it here at home with everyone around- it also ruins the surprise about what my monologue is about. I'm not completely satisfied with the script, but I'm always super picky about stuff I write.

Maybe one day I'll appreciate my scars.

So I Don't Lose My Head   04-15-2007

I avoid updating like I avoid everything. The monologue went well the first night but I stumbled on lines the second night. No one says it was noticeable, but I was emotionally worn out by the second night.

Reactions? All positive. But not about my acting- they were all about me. The two comments I've heard dominantly are "bold" and "beautiful". The more I think about those remarks, the more I wonder how those thoughts would come to in anyone's head.

They say: "You're beautiful".
They mean: "*I can't imagine having to wake up every morning to what you do. As a good friend I should give you as much confidence/ support as possible.*"

184

Result: Nice gesture, but it is easy to say as a third party. I can't believe it is possible. Reversing the situation, would you think that you are beautiful? Far from. It's harsh to say, but it's almost condescending because of the fact that we both know it isn't true and if you and I were both scarred, we'd do anything to reverse the damage.

They say: *"That was bold "*.

They mean: *"It's known that if you are to show your true self onstage looking the way you do, lots of people are going to be thankful that they don't look like you. So in a way, we're all judging you, because none of us (in our right minds) would want those abnormalities"*.

Result: Who would want that burden? To wake up every day to look in the mirror and see what I see?

Dr. A and I have been on better terms. Two appointments ago she made me cry near the end of the session because I was so frustrated; it was as if every word I said to her got lost while traveling in the air without ever making it to her ears. She told me I'm more genuine and not "coy" when I'm crying and talking but I also have a bad habit of minimizing my emotional accomplishments. I have an appointment tomorrow with her, so it looks like she's booking me weekly now.

I told her that my main concern is finding a way to get rid of the urge to pick. It comes so naturally now, as it has for years… it's just like breathing. When I don't pick, my mind starts suffocating, going into overdrive just gasping for that release. She still thinks that by reducing my Borderline symptoms everything will start falling into place because I can then find other outlets for my OCD tendency to pick. She's the fourth therapist person to declare that I have Borderline, so it's pretty well confirmed. She said I have almost all the criteria to diagnose it. Sometimes I feel like I'm wasting my time with therapy and that I should go out to work but every time I do that, I get worse. Then I feel like I'm going to get worse no matter what and it's what I do with my down in the dumps that'll be the best time of my life.

Modeling? 05-03-2007

Just a quick update:

I went modeling about a week ago. I asked for all pictures to be touched up before I get them back. I don't know if I have the guts to post pictures online of me all scarred up because photos, unlike acting, are stills... evidence... and permanent. I also want to see myself from another point of view because when I look at myself I just can't see past the scars.

21 TOMORROW! 05-25-2007

Tomorrow, May 26th, is my 21st birthday. I feel really old now and so unaccomplished. I wanted to be places by now; I wanted to be happy, to be settled with someone, be finishing University/ college, and/ or be out on my own. These are goals that I haven't even nearly come close to completing because I'm so wrapped up in my own problems to move my head past my rut.

In total for this month, I've been to 3 photo shoots. It's something I never thought I'd have the guts to do, but I'm testing my limits and pushing my boundaries just so I can get to a healthy medium of acceptance about who I am. Whenever I get back touched-up pictures back along with the original copies, I praise the art that can be made using photo retouching programs to remove my scars.

For the past two months my ankles have been picked raw. Usually picking doesn't hurt but for some reason my ankles have been so sore and the time I shaved (*not often*) it felt like the new razor was ripping the skin off of my body. I have a bit of an infection on my left knee which worried me before I went to sleep yesterday. I actually have a few but this one bothered me the most. They're caused by the material of my velvety pajamas sticking to opened wounds. I had a dream was that I was downtown and I looked down at my leg [I was wearing shorts]; above my left knee was about a 4 x 7 inch hunk of skin removed. Beneath all of the removed layers there were still scars and I was bleeding everywhere. God, my unconscious self needs therapy!

Back to the photo shoot, after getting the photos back I've been on a more natural high feeling better about myself despite knowing that yes, photo shop makes me look like a normal human being. In the last two days, I got messages from both of my mom's sisters (who do not speak to each other) saying that I need to eat because I look too skinny. I'm pissed. They both live provinces away and this was the crap I went through with my grandfather growing up. It reminds me of the constant abuse of being compared to my sister; about how chubby I was, how my

187

face was ugly and scarred, how I wasn't as smart as her, and how I should be more like her because she'll be successful... even in the love department. At one time I was too chubby (when I was a kid) and now I'm too skinny? I'll never win.

When It's Terrifying to Be Yourself...   06-24-2007

Online, I came across a video called "Dermatillomania". In it, a man was showing how he is a skin picker and he showed his ritual to the camera, explaining the high that he gets from picking spots he finds.

It wasn't the video that scared me, but there were over 20 pages of comments with most of them telling the guy he's sick, disgusting, just "shouldn't do it", is a freak, telling him to wear a band aid, etc. It's mortifying to see this kind of feedback... and so much of it; makes me want to hide in a hole somewhere far away...

It's fucking downright ignorance with people saying what they don't have the balls to say to someone in real life.

Long Time No Update   08-07-2007

I've been pretty disappointed in myself for the past 2 months, although I've been trying to hide it. I ended up getting a major chin infection that was most likely caused by my skin picking. I've been putting off this update because there's so much to say about what's happened since then, but I'll try to make it brief and to the point.

To me, it's obvious that I'm a picker so I didn't want to go to the medical centre to get a finger-wag from the doctor, but there was none of that so I got a cream and left. The infection and swelling died down after a few days, but my chin isn't quite the same. I thought that it just healed the wrong way because of the trauma that was done to it. I haven't told anyone this part, but yesterday I ripped it open because I was tired of it being huge and all of this pus kept coming out with very "pop" I did so, my chin looks severe again. The infection was never actually cured- it went dormant. I returned home from the medical centre a few hours ago and there was a nice doctor who told me that it's time for some strong oral anti-biotics. She asked me how old I was and I told her 21- she looked puzzled when I gave her that answer. She said that while I was there, she could make a prescription to clear up my acne. When I refused she looked taken back and she said that people are usually self conscious about it, but I told her I was ok with it. Hahaha- I didn't want to explain my history with this disorder with her. Seeing that my dermatologist told me during my skin treatments a couple of years ago that I only have about 5% acne, it just wasn't worth the time explaining.

The 1st infection just happened to start growing two visits ago with Dr. A [El Bitcho]. I told her about it in my next appointment and, get this; she told me that I did it to myself purposely because I was upset that she had booked me a month ahead instead of the normal two weeks ahead since she was on vacation. WHAT??? In her eyes, it was that she had abandoned me and I took it out on myself. First of all, it's an obvious load of bullshit because I hate going to see her and still don't trust her. Secondly, the timeline doesn't add up because this happened before the rebooking took place. This angers me to no end and I was supposed to have an appointment with her a few days ago, but I went the day *after* by accident. It took three bus rides to get there when she could have called the day before asking why I didn't show up.

I'm also now on a low dosage of a common mood-stabilizer which seems to actually be reducing the picking just a tiny bit. By looking at my face right now you wouldn't be able to tell because the infection is making these really weird and disgusting zits along my jaw line. Maybe it's my imagination that it was getting better before I brought out the infection, which I'm telling people that I picked it *after* it started growing again.

I have a minor crush on a boy. Boy has a crush on me and has since over a year and a half ago. Boy confesses then goes back home to the USA after finishing his degree here. I pushed him away back then because my confidence was significantly lower than it is now- I didn't even feel human back then. We met up again through another mutual friend this February. Anyway, where I'm getting with this, is last night when I talked about my infection (he knows about the disorder and has seen my scars) and how I'm not leaving the house except to go to the doctor's.

He said to me:

"Ang, you could lose all of your hair and your body could be completely burned and you'd still be beautiful"

Damn it, haha. It's bittersweet for me that now I like him and ruined my chances before. It gives me some peace that not all guys out there are immature chicken shits... unless all of the Canadian boys are.

190

For the most part, everything has been mediocre lately. My chin has flared up for a 3rd time, which was yet again my fault. The infection stayed dormant like last time and when I saw the results of my modeling pictures, I noticed how my chin is much more round and plump than what it used to be. Of course I'm the only one able to notice it; to everyone else it just looks... normal. I knew it wasn't, so a few days ago I said I would be done with this hibernating infection once and for all.

I poked at it with a bulletin board pin several times three days ago and was able to peel off the first scabbing layer today. Of course, two photographers have randomly contacted me in these past few days for shoots. Fuck. I'm postponing/ stalling for the time being.

I created a website to bring about awareness to this disorder, but I only have one voice that goes as far as my network/ realm. I'm so thankful that 76 people have joined the cause thus far but I can't help but think that it will only reach 100 because people I know won't invite anyone. I want to raise hell and make this a shit storm. If people I know are able to recruit 20 others then actual awareness will be reached other than with only people who know my dirty laundry.

I graced Dr. A with my presence yesterday, which went over very differently than any other appointment. After I told her off/ confronted her at our last visit, she changed her whole approach with me. She's being too kind, blowing bubbles up my ass by telling me that I'm wise, intelligent, overly- responsible, etc. *Finally* we're going to start some sort of habit reversal therapy where, starting today, I have to record every time I pick, why I did it, what I was doing beforehand, and how I picked

191

to understand a pattern. I have to do this for two weeks. When I went to see her, I wore a scarf to cover the bandage on my chin; very alerting for people in warm weather to look over and see a chick wearing a scarf. Smooooooth.

Dear "Television Psychologist",   07-14-2008

"*I'm Angie, 22, and from Canada. I suffer from Dermatillomania, the compulsive skin picking disorder. More people have heard of Trichotillomania, the hair pulling disorder and this is what I was diagnosed as having since the DSM doesn't recognize Dermatillomania as a separate disorder. Your show with the woman who has fiber coming out of her skin triggered me to write this because of the shame she must feel about having the marks on her body that she does. I've been picking at my skin my whole life, but it got out of control... meaning I had more visible marks which made me take drastic measures to hide, all of this started when I was 13. From that time until I was 18, I thought I was the only person to have this problem, something freakish I made myself. I avoid social situations which may reveal the current condition of my skin on bad days and though I'm open about having this disorder, it's hard to talk to friends about in the now but easier to talk about past situations with my disorder.*

I can give you a quick glimpse about what I've looked like since I was 13. About 50% of my body is covered in that, which includes my back, shoulders, upper chest, upper arms, lower back, and legs. I would love to be able to speak open about it on the show for the most exposure about this problem that many people have. My goal to spread the awareness comes from wanting to prevent people from feeling what I did in those 5 lonely years. I've been recruiting people a cause online and it's been rewarding to get messages from strangers thanking me for being the person to tell them

192

that they're not alone.

Spreading the awareness has been the only outlet from isolation I have.
Helping others which in turn, help me."

And Again...   *10-14-2007*

Well, I went through Round Four of disgusting facial infection,
except it's now traveled in between my eyes. I went to the medical centre
today to get anti-biotics for it and instead of getting treated, I got a
lecture, backed into a corner, talked down to, the "*you shouldn't have done it
to yourself anyway so you'll have to tough it out*", and a literal light slap on the
hand from the doctor when I rested my hand on my face out of
frustration when all I wanted to do was smack him. I couldn't confront
him because I know I would have started bawling my eyes out. He sat
right in front of my face with his glasses at the tip of his nose, head
lowered, and eyes raised while using a baby voice with me.

I'd say the consult lasted between 5 and 7 minutes even though it
felt like a good half hour. Those are the type of visits I get panicky about;
luckily, the last few times the doctors have been willing to treat the issue
an understanding doctor. He condescendingly asked me if I thought he
was crazy when he told me that life is good. I answered with a short,
"No". He told me not to pick at myself then. Fucking moron.

Went home and was cursing up a storm, using I don't say in the
house. I just felt so humiliated, and all these weird things came into my
head so I just tried to sleep it off after I cried into my pillow for a good
half hour. The nap worked, but I feel so... I don't know really. I'd rather

193

not write out everything the doofus said in there, but that's an outline. Nonetheless I'm not going anywhere for a few days, until I don't look like I was beaten the hell out of.

- CONCLUSION -

I am not a scholar, a writer, or an expert on any mental illness. I am just a twenty three year old young woman who has suffered from skin picking for most of her life. By reading my journal I got to explore myself and see how far I've come in the last few years. After reviewing what I've written three years after the fact, I am shocked that I survived dealing with my self-hate. I was forced to bring myself back to the days when I believed that I couldn't reverse that I permanently screwed up my life and death was always optional as a fix.

Am I hopeless in regards to being cured of this disorder? It would be a lie if I said that the answer is most likely a no; most mental illnesses are diagnosed through psychiatric evaluations, not by hard scientific fact. There are no blood tests to determine who has depression, no recognized gene to determine if a child will grow up and be plagued with obsessive-compulsive disorder. Dermatillomania is far behind any mental illness in terms of awareness or even acceptability amongst society. This needs to change because dermatologists are giving false diagnoses with skin disorders and some mental health professionals are not even open to the idea that such a compulsion even exists.

Acting was the profession I wanted to go into, despite knowing that I could never do it because of my scars. Correction: not 'never', but it would be very demanding and it wasn't a challenge I wanted to pursue. I tried to find meaning in my life by living like everyone else does by finding a profession so I could ultimately grow into an independent young woman. Despite having some passion in the theatrical realm, I lacked the motivation to take the necessary steps required to be a success in that field. In the end, I became sick of playing "make believe" and desired to seek out a profession that delved into hard truths instead of fluttering around in a fantasy world. Not meaning to disrespect the theatre world by any means, but it was not for me and I could not make a clear distinction between theatre and life without yearning for facts, perspectives, and reality.

Modeling was supposed to be a one-time deal as a way to see myself from another person's perspective and to see what I would look like without scars once the post work was done to the images. After my first shoot, I was contacted by a handful of photographers and have been modeling ever since. For me, it's been a way to learn how to accept myself without conventionally sitting in an 8x8 room with a professional holding onto every word I say. It appears contradictory to some people that I send out a message to be happy with yourself, yet I get perfected images of myself taken. First and foremost, do what inspires you; it's nice to take that step outside of yourself and see that you are already on the covers of magazines. Those images in the media of flawless bodies are fake; it's easier to accept that it is impossible to strive to look like airbrushed images when the model herself isn't perfect. A rippling effect took place from modeling and I got into makeup artistry, also as a pastime. I had an option of becoming a licensed makeup artist for a career but I needed something mentally challenging and real. Modeling has not cured my insecurity with having these scars. I am still very self conscious about them and deep down, still blame myself for being the cause of them.

After taking two years off from school to recover from the thoughts that tipped me over the edge, I realized that I was lucky to be alive and gained a strong will to succeed. When I reread these documented struggles I became embarrassed that I was once so convinced that I had failed in life without it even starting. I decided to enroll in another post-secondary institution- one that offered a Child & Youth Care program. I was offered another chance at life that many other kids need guidance in finding; I knew that I had the compassion, intuition, problem-solving skills, sensitivity, and openness to assist a youth in trouble. However, going to that school was the most expensive mistake of my life that will take a good decade to recover from financially.

In the first three months there, I was placed with groups of people from other programs to complete the mandatory courses that were needed to get a diploma. I interacted well with everyone, like I had in any of my jobs, in high school, and in university. Sure, not everyone is best friends with one another, but you find who you connect with and don't bother to carry on with who you do not. Once I entered the Child & Youth Care classroom, I was the new kid who exempted one of the mandatory courses because of my university experience… and I immediately became a target to people who lack the insight needed to be in this profession.

Before I could put names and faces together, I heard what a group of girls were saying about me and saw things that they falsely posted remarks about me online. The dirty looks and whispers was something I was not used to, so I made an announcement one day that I would not tolerate such asinine behavior. It may not have been the wisest choice of mine, but it was one that carried heavy repercussions for the next nine months that I endured the harassment. For adults to be acting this way is unacceptable, but for adults who are becoming role models for youth... is this the ignorance that the future holds for them? Another method I used was to tell everyone in the class about my Dermatillomania in an open forum because I knew if I didn't, I would not be able to handle the ridicule about something that hurts my heart so deeply; I knew that the main culprits of this behavior constantly made fun of other's appearances, so I would be a walking pin cushion of intimidations.

Things got worse as time went on, but my first one-on-one incident happened when I went to the washroom during class and was followed by an older woman. I had said something in class the day before that pushed boundaries and I apologized right before going to the washroom because I never mean to offend anyone with my very bold statements. When I went to wash my hands, she stood right behind me and had me cornered. At first she proceeded to tell me that it wasn't appropriate to say what I did, but then it quickly turned to accusations such as me using my disorder as a reason why people don't like me. That comment was a blow to who I am, what I stand for, and I burst into tears because I was appalled that someone could even suggest that. Then she told me that I made some sort of inappropriate comment about the rape of a ten year old from a case study of ours; there is no way in hell that I would even come near making a joke or any sarcastic comment about a child's torture. If I had made a vile comment, why not call me out on it during the open forum? If I had heard someone make any inappropriate comments regarding that topic, I would have pointed it out right away. That's what made me differ from many of the students in that class- I was not a coward.

From that moment on, I did not feel safe in that school. The administration proceeded to make excuses, saying that "people will have their disagreements". My request to file a formal complaint was downright denied with no explanation. As the months passed by, the banter grew out of control. Friends of these girls were disgusted with them for what they were doing to me daily, yet they didn't want to become targets by sticking up for me. Standing up for myself was hard because I am obviously going to be bias but I'm the type of person who will stick up for someone being bullied, even if it meant ever standing up for the woman who cornered me in the washroom. By becoming authority figures that are helping to shape struggling youth's lives, we need to fight injustices for a greater good. We need to be role models and not purposely hurt others because youth pick up on the attitudes and beliefs a worker has. If you cannot treat your colleague with respect, even if you hate her guts, how do you expect to be a positive influence on a child?

We wasted a lot of time in class by listening to how each other's nights went. An hour and a half of drinking stories was not what I was paying for, yet students would become histrionic the minute I would open my mouth to discuss, or even challenge, an academic topic that the instructor covered. A few people have said that I am annoying in doing so and should believe what the teacher says. In a field regarding human behavior, I refuse to believe one opinion without raising other questions; I think for myself and take perspectives, cultures, dynamics, socio-economic statuses, etc. into account when making a decision. What will these people do when they have to make an independent decision during a crisis without a supervisor around to instruct them?

One day, I did a power point presentation on Trichotillomania. I went into the details about the differences between it and Dermatillomania, but how the DSM doesn't recognize the latter as a disorder of its own. I admittedly included pictures I found of sufferers online who have these disorders, along with two of my own. When I finished my presentation, the room was dead silent. Then one of the girls spouted out in front of the class, *"Man, I'm surprised I kept my lunch down after seeing those pictures"*. I was furious and told her that it wasn't appropriate, and her friend backed her up by saying that it was my fault, that I should have given a warning about graphic images before I started. I agreed that maybe I should have, but I see these scars everyday and have to live with them- this is normal to me and God forbid they meet a kid like me in their future endeavors. Unfortunately, the kid would have that memory etched in her mind forever, while it would be only a fleeting moment for them. I spoke with another classmate in the washroom who agreed with me that it was wrong for her to say and I told her that it is people like her that have driven me to release this book.

I had to report these girls to the office many times, and in return I would get nothing back. I had proof of many incidents, including ones that occurred right in front of the teacher, but I had no one to back me up. Slowly I went into a depression, but didn't realize it because I was not having suicidal thoughts; every time I have been depressed in the past, suicidal ideations were the warning flags that told me I needed help. This time around, I crashed at an exponential rate. I was slurring my words, couldn't hold a conversation without losing my train of thought, lost seconds of my day, and was seeing things at times that weren't there. It was like reality was only in fragments and in the seconds I lost, I didn't know what was going on around me. Never in my teen or adult years have I been targeted by such immaturity and hate. Elementary and early junior high schools were struggles, but kids were not determined to hurt me then- they just said stupid and random things that hurt more than they could comprehend at the time. I ended up leaving because of the administration that did nothing but give general "professionalism" speeches to the class, followed by blowing bubbles up the their asses by dismissing the bad behavior and focusing on the positive behavior. How are we (the students) supposed to come out of our shells by doing what's right when the staff wouldn't? To that school, I was one paycheck that they could afford to lose over the few who do not have the capacity to behave past the pre-teen years. Not once were those girls addressed, let alone disciplined, for their actions.

It took until one spontaneous day in January of 2009 to start dating again after I spontaneously took a chance. After being single for so many years something in me just thought, "why the hell not?" I avoided dating or any form of intimacy because I felt that I looked so disgusting and that it was my fault that I am the way I am; no decent male in his right mind would want to get close to the mess that's in my head… or on my skin. Something strange inside of me told me to trust my gut instinct of getting close to the man I met, that he was a rare kind of special that prompted an immediate attraction.

It was nearly four years to the date since I had even kissed anyone else, and the last time was when I was almost raped. Getting involved with someone romantically wasn't even in my vocabulary, but something told me that it was safe and even if things didn't work out between him and I because of my issues, then I wouldn't lose much because I wouldn't have gotten close enough to him for it to matter. One night I was lying in his (Barrett's) arms and said to him, *"You know… it's my fault that I have these scars"*. His unexpected reaction was, *"It's not your fault… there are some things people can't control"*. I quickly shot up in surprise because I didn't tell him why I was scarred up and he told me that he found information on me online relating to this disorder. I was terrified to tell him, but it didn't matter because he already knew. He didn't care why or how they got there; it wasn't an issue for him. Barrett was able to see past years of scarring to notice that I was someone that he could enjoy being with.

From the moment that I laid eyes on this man, I knew that he would play an important role in my life. He had a slightly nervous demeanor about him which disappeared after a few minutes in the coffee shop where we met. The crystal blue of his eyes showed a lot of soul, but it was his boyish smile that captivated me. After an ambiguous, yet fulfilling eight months, it became clear that he felt a disconnect he did not want in a relationship. I do not regret our time together or many of my naïve choices in the relationship because a gap has been filled. I am worthy of being cared for, I deserve to be loved, and I need a communicative partner who can appreciate me for all of my qualities. Although I was not looking for a learning experience, I figured out that I am capable of loving a man as a romantic partner, but now I deserve to know what it's like to be loved in return.

My friends and family have been nothing but supportive during these rough times- I just didn't know how to connect with them and let them be there for me. One thing I learned is that I did not give them enough credit, which is still an ongoing battle with me. They may not understand what it's like to be in my shoes, but they accept me for my faults because they love me; there's not much that I can tell them that would push them away for good (trust me, I've tried as a defense mechanism). At heart, I am still an introverted loner who prefers solitude over a night out with friends so I can do my own thing. There is nothing wrong with being this way, but I still struggle with balancing my social life to let my close handful of friends know that I treasure what they give to me daily.

My chin never fully healed from the infection I had a couple of years ago. After many visits to the dermatologist about its enlargement, he concluded that there is no longer an infection; it's internal scar tissue damage. While trying to get it diagnosed there was a possibility that I had a form of skin cancer. Growing up, our parents tend to our scrapes by washing them, applying anti-biotic creams, and bandage them to make sure they heal correctly. By picking my skin on a daily basis I am always at risk of another infection like this or even one that can travel to my bloodstream. If I took the time to execute a proper cleaning regime every time I picked, I would be in the washroom for most of my days. These days my chin is still enlarged enough for me to notice it. If I laugh too hard or cry too much, the muscles along my chin become too tired to maintain the facial gesture. What I learned about myself from having this infection attack my skin is that I'm not indestructible. There are dangers to my every day life, from dirt under my nails to an un-sanitized "tool" that I use to pick with.

Giving advice is usually easy for me to do, with my logical personality, but when it comes to this disorder I don't know what to tell others. I am too cynical about overcoming this disorder because it has taken on its own personality within me; my moods no longer reflect the severity of my picking because my skin has been clearer during some dark times than when things are going my way. I contribute my mentally healthier well-being to the anti-depressants that I am still taking; I have been on the same ones for three years now and they have worked on my depression just like they did for me in grade twelve. If I were to give hope to another Dermatillomania sufferer about the prognosis of this disorder, I'd be a little more optimistic than I am for myself because it manifests differently for each person. For some people it may be treated as OCD while other people need extensive talk therapy, which includes cognitive behavioral therapy. There are so many factors surrounding one's outcome with this illness that I cannot say everyone who has it is doomed to it for the rest of their lives.

For non-believers of mental health issues, I cannot stress enough what an ill mind can do to a person's quality of life. Other than the apparent emotional drawbacks it has, the toll it can take on a person's body is incredible. When I went into the last documented depression after coming off of my old medication, my anxiety was at an all-time high. The daily diarrhea it triggered caused my weight to drop to an all-time low of 119Lbs, which is not healthy for a woman who is 5'9 with a medium build. The low dosage of a mood stabilizer I went on slowly brought my weight up; I was able to keep food in and enjoy many tastes all over again. After a few months, I decided to step on a scale after a pair of pants couldn't fit anymore and I laughed when the scale read 157Lbs... but that laughter turned into a bit of a panic after I confirmed with my family that our scale was correct. For more than a year now, I have maintained a weight of 145Lbs (give or take a few pounds) and I wouldn't care if I stayed like this for the rest of my life.

My appointments with Dr. A came to an abrupt stop after a session where we were trying to deal with my Dermatillomania. I worked relentlessly to complete the homework I was assigned out of an OCD workbook only to have her say that I wasn't ready to stop picking. She offered no explanation and it was her second time trying to pass me off, so I decided to not return because I was just being run around in circles. I do not contribute my healthier mindset from her; she was always quick to judge and put me down, which led me to some of my lowest moments. The day treatment program taught me many skills related to self esteem and self worth which came into play naturally as time progressed. I now only see my psychiatrist once every few months to make sure that the pills I'm on are still working well with my body.

I have finally acknowledged that I will always have this disorder. It took a blow to my pride to bow down and admit that I will have to live with this forever, but it has also given me a chance to move past the feeling of being a failure. I had to stop giving myself the unrealistic expectation of quitting this compulsion because it would send me into too much of a depressive tailspin when I wouldn't succeed. By accepting that I will have this disorder forever, I have been able to move on in my life and focus on improving my social interactions and lifestyle. In the back of my mind I will always hope that medical advances will help find a way to eliminate the urge to pick my own skin. Then a small question comes up in my mind- if I could be completely rid of this disorder with a pill, would I take it? We all know that I would in a flash, but I will admit that Dermatillomania has become a part of my identity and a part of me would find it challenging to part with.

As for the day treatment program, I have not heard from Tony since October of 2006. Eventually, everyone I kept in some contact with from the program just trailed back into their own lives. It's hard for someone who has never been in a program like this to understand that in such a short time, you become like a little supportive family with the other out- patients because you've shared secrets that you may never have even acknowledged before. The environment was a fantasy land where you could tell anyone anything without being judged. I believe that the main difficulty with staying friends with everyone in a program like this is that they embody the most painful time of your life, which makes it easier to move onto healthier choices without that reminder of what was. I would be overjoyed to hear from any of them today; they gave me the gift of trust and accepted me for everything that I was at that point in my life. Most of the patients were in their forties and fifties, but they never talked down to me like "the kid" of the program- I was their equal.

I vented, ranted, and raved in this journal so often that keeping names out of many entries was necessary. A few of my friends have told me that they do not care if their name pops up, but petty arguments and disagreements from three years ago do not need to resurface to show readers how each of my friends tick. In reality, I am not a role model. So far I have failed at completing any post-secondary education pursuit; I still live at home, and don't know how to get a life of my own started. Unlike before, I now have so many goals that it's difficult to stay focused on one in order to achieve it. Although I may have spoiled my chance to ever be financially stable enough to finish my Child & Youth Care program online, it hasn't stopped me from keeping it in the back of my mind. Some goals now include getting a place of my own, make a decent living, maybe get into photography while continuing to model and do makeup for people. Other thoughts are getting back into playing the flute and piccolo in a full ensemble, getting back into theatre as a pastime, learning how to drive a car, learning how to play a saxophone, and upgrade my prehistoric means of technology little by little. My zealous need to live has prompted me to create a bucket list of over 50 goals I want to achieve before I die, from riding a horse on a dirt road to successfully making squeaking noises by blowing into a blade of grass.

While those are near future goals I have been considering, completing this document has been my top priority since leaving school. I made the decision in December of 2008 to turn my journal into a book because I realized that I had overcome my destructive days and I was ready to turn my experiences into something that someone else with this disorder can benefit from. Even if you do not suffer from Dermatillomania the heart of the matter focuses on depression, although the root of mine was this disorder. While writing these entries, I would have loved to have a book in my possession about someone's experience with skin picking and how it affected his or her life; I firmly believe that my need to connect with someone who has this was overwhelmingly strong and because I didn't, it made it much easier to sink into isolation.

It is a risk to have this document in the hands of people in my life because it may only reach their eyes instead of also reaching the eyes of someone who can benefit mentally from this. In any case, this was something I had to do for myself as a "pay it forward" for surviving my suicidal days. I yearn to express my newfound attitudes on life to the world to avoid more lives being destroyed by ignorance and loneliness. No matter what backlash I face from exposing this dirty little secret, I am more than ready for it. I need to stay true to myself by standing up for what I believe in, even if it means standing alone.